TRUST AS THE CORE

OF INSTRUCTIONAL LEADERSHIP

Protocols to
Mediate Thinking,
Shift Practice, &
Improve Student Learning

DELIA E. RACINES

Solution Tree | Press

a division of
Solution Tree

555 North Morton Street
Bloomington, IN 47404
800.733.6786 (toll free) / 812.336.7700
FAX: 812.336.7790

email: info@SolutionTree.com
SolutionTree.com

Visit **go.SolutionTree.com/leadership** to download the free reproducibles in this book.

Printed in the United States of America

Library of Congress Cataloging-in-Publication Data

Names: Racines, Delia E., author.
Title: Trust as the core of instructional leadership : protocols to mediate
  thinking, shift practice, and improve student learning / Delia E.
  Racines.
Description: Bloomington, IN : Solution Tree Press, 2022. | Includes
  bibliographical references and index.
Identifiers: LCCN 2021061777 (print) | LCCN 2021061778 (ebook) | ISBN
  9781951075545 (paperback) | ISBN 9781949539370 (ebook)
Subjects: LCSH: Teacher-student relationships. | Teaching--Psychological
  aspects. | School environment.
Classification: LCC LB1033 .R2824 2022 (print) | LCC LB1033 (ebook) | DDC
  371.102/3--dc23/eng/20220124
LC record available at https://lccn.loc.gov/2021061777
LC ebook record available at https://lccn.loc.gov/2021061778

Solution Tree
Jeffrey C. Jones, CEO
Edmund M. Ackerman, President

Solution Tree Press
President and Publisher: Douglas M. Rife
Associate Publisher: Sarah Payne-Mills
Managing Production Editor: Kendra Slayton
Editorial Director: Todd Brakke
Art Director: Rian Anderson
Copy Chief: Jessi Finn
Content Development Specialist: Amy Rubenstein
Acquisitions Editor: Sarah Jubar
Text and Cover Designer: Abigail Bowen
Associate Editor and Proofreader: Sarah Ludwig
Editorial Assistants: Charlotte Jones and Elijah Oates

To my beautiful parents. Thank you for teaching me the most about being trustworthy, trusting others, and trusting myself.

ACKNOWLEDGMENTS

There are so many people I would like to thank for their unwavering support throughout the development of this book.

First and foremost, to my gems of parents. Thank you for always supporting each and every crazy dream I have that somehow comes to fruition. You are there at every turn I drastically take, and I am most grateful for your belief that I can do anything I set my mind to. Thanks, Mom and Dad. To my brother, Jorge: thank you for supporting me no matter what—from moving me into college during parent week to cheering me on during every major and minor accomplishment since.

To my better half, Nathan Bryan (and our beloved four-legged son, Guillermo Felipe). Thank you for listening to every chapter, edit, and idea I had for this book. You have attended every in-person and virtual conference and helped me prepare for and travel to every presentation throughout my career. Thanks for always logging into my virtual conferences from the garage with Guillermo to make sure everything is good to go every time! I appreciate your support, particularly when I was a principal during COVID-19; I would not have made it without your calmness and camera support. Thank you for always listening to and believing in my dreams to improve the field, if only by a tiny millimeter.

A big thank-you—and GIF in the form of a big hug—to Sarah Jubar. Thank you for all your valuable time and thoughtful edits to make sure this book is exactly what I hoped for it to be: a helpful resource for all current and aspiring instructional leaders to establish trust in schools. Thank you to every single person at Solution Tree who had a hand in bringing this book to life. I appreciate the countless hours and careful attention you dedicated to every detail. From the beginning of my teaching career, Solution Tree has always been such a supportive resource for me. It is a complete dream to have now written a resource *for* Solution Tree. Thank you, thank you, thank you!

I owe a special thank-you to the individuals who shared their stories about trust in education for the Educator Spotlight component of this book: Jess Dove, Melissa Trout, Rae Mitchell, Lourdes "Lulu" Amador, Breána Victoria, Ann Delehant, Nadya Briggs, Brittany Hott, Kendra Chapman, Melissa Ferro, and April Cage. I appreciate your thoughtful contributions; all the laughs, learning, and stories throughout the years; and, most important, our friendship. I value each coaching conversation we have had throughout this process, and I am confident the experiences you each shared will inspire readers to value their own journeys and build a foundation of trust in schools to improve student learning.

To Jim Knight, the guru of instructional coaching, whom I had the great opportunity to chat with in Vancouver—of course, without my knowing that Nathan had sat down with you, unaware you were *the* Jim Knight! Thank you for including me in your book and for always being a model coach to so many educators around the world. Coaching changes lives, and your research and Jim Knightisms in particular make a significant difference; they certainly have for me.

To the supportive mentors I am so blessed to have in my life: Frank Jenkins, Kate O'Connor, Lynn Hill, and Nancy Fehrle, as well as Jackie Rossell and John Uncles (may you both rest in peace—I know you two are pulling some serious strings up there!). Thank you for always finding the time to give me wise advice and for being pillars of trust in my life. Thank you for your genuine friendship and support.

I am eternally grateful for each of you. Thank you.

Solution Tree Press would like to thank the following reviewers:

Heather Bell-Williams
Principal
Milltown Elementary School
Anglophone South School District
St. Stephen, New Brunswick, Canada

Kati Boland
Principal
Fulton High School
Fulton, Missouri

Laura Hesson
Washington County School District
    Board Member
Washington County School District
St. George, Utah

Salma Hussein
Assistant Principal
Central Senior High School
Saint Paul, Minnesota

Jed Kees
Principal
Onalaska Middle School
Onalaska, Wisconsin

Benjamin Kitslaar
Principal
West Side Elementary
Elkhorn, Wisconsin

Jennifer Steele
Assistant Principal
Northside High School
Fort Smith, Arkansas

Ringnolda Jofee' Tremain
K–8 Principal
Texas Leadership Charter Academy
San Angelo, Texas

Visit **go.SolutionTree.com/leadership** to download the free reproducibles in this book.

TABLE OF CONTENTS

Reproducible pages are in italics.

ABOUT THE AUTHOR

 **Delia E. Racines, PhD,** serves as an administrator overseeing a Reading and Literacy Added Authorization Program as well as a School Business Management Certificate Program, is an adjunct professor, and serves as a consultant in Los Angeles, California. She has served as a principal, assistant principal, instructional coach, and teacher over the past seventeen years. Racines has built instructional coaching programs from the ground up, led various professional development initiatives, and aligned efforts with each district's progress as professional learning communities to ensure equitable opportunities and outcomes for all students.

Racines effectively transitioned department chairs to instructional coaches through tailored modules and received Learning Forward's prestigious Shirley Hord Learning Team Award. Racines also designs and delivers courses and professional development with the University of Southern California Rossier School of Education's Office of Professional Development for matriculating MAT-TESOL students, Endicott College, and Teaching Matters. For her research in education law and civil rights for English learners, she received the Emerald Literati Award for Outstanding Author Contribution. Racines was nominated for the Association of California School Administrators' Co-Administrator of the Year and received the Teachers Honoring Excellence Award for 2018–2019 in Los Angeles.

Racines received a bachelor's degree in sociology from Virginia Tech, a master's degree in criminology from Radford University, and both a master's degree in curriculum and instruction in multilingual multicultural education and a doctorate in teacher education and educational leadership from George Mason University.

To learn more about Racines's work, visit www.frominsighttoequity.com, @frominsighttoequity on Instagram, and @Dr_D_R on Twitter.

To book Delia E. Racines for professional development, contact pd@SolutionTree.com.

INTRODUCTION

Consider these facts: according to researchers Kara S. Finnigan and Alan J. Daly (2017), educator Teresa Rensch (2019), and professor of educational leadership Megan Tschannen-Moran (2014), high levels of trust in schools correspond to high levels of performance in both teacher and student learning. In fact, writes Jon Saphier (2018), founder and president of Research for Better Teaching, "School leadership literature repeatedly identifies trust as essential for creating high-gain schools—schools where student [outcomes equate to] more than one year's worth of achievement at a given grade level" (p. 14). Findings from studies conducted by professors Patrick B. Forsyth, Curt M. Adams, and Wayne K. Hoy (2011) similarly show that colleagues' trust in one another and trust in leadership are positively correlated with student achievement. And in the most effective leadership situations—those in which all members of the team trust one another—employees are more likely to be happy, engaged, and innovative, explains Karyn Twaronite (2016) of the *Harvard Business Review*.

Trust, of course, is not something that develops on its own, even when people have the best of intentions and access to, or knowledge of, research-based leadership and instructional strategies. Oftentimes, suggestions for improving trust begin and end with that simple directive: that is, they leave much to be desired in terms of exactly *where* to begin, or explicit instructions on *what* to do. Even otherwise strong research, such as that of Forsyth and colleagues (2011), that seeks to identify how leadership generates collective trust may include rather general, open-ended recommendations to "make authentic behavior and openness habits of action" and "confirm collaborative and professional behavior as the norm," as well as put an emphasis on principals (p. 173). Indeed, scales and surveys used to measure trust in schools often include questions regarding satisfaction and relationships with the principal, or they'll ask respondents to rate the principal (Forsyth et al., 2011). While principals are central to a school environment that promotes trust, *all* school leaders impact staff's practices and are responsible for creating, sustaining, and fostering trust, according to researchers Geert Devos, Melissa Tuytens, and Hester Hulpia (2014); Benjamin Kutsyuruba, Keith Walker, and Brian Noonan (2016); and Douglas Wieczorek and Jeffrey Lear (2018). All school leaders are, in fact, instructional leaders and are essential in creating a shared commitment to a school's development and developing or building capacity in the educators that serve our students. But they must be equipped with the knowledge and tools to undertake and sustain the work. In this book, we'll explore the development of this knowledge and these tools by way of five key trust-building practices that I advocate: (1) be visible and approachable; (2) listen closely to the complaint for a request; (3) invite all voices; (4) use a strengths-based approach toward building instructional leadership capacity; and (5) unpack necessary conversations with care. But first, let's review the most important components of trust, who will most benefit from the book, and the book's structure.

Trust Defined

As we know from firsthand experience, trust does not equate to simply words and their meanings; it is also often dependent on a recall of exchanges from very specific, vivid scenarios of what people did or did not do. It may even rely on those powerful, intuitive gut feelings that we have about people. In their studies of various fields, experts agree on several concrete components of trust, and it is these commonalities across definitions that we'll consider in our discussions of trust throughout the book.

- **Competence:** Frequently cited in literature on trust is the essential quality of competence. Referencing the work of Stephen Covey, educational researcher Michael Fullan (2014) explains that behaviors matter, and that trust must be modeled in one's day-to-day actions; people must be not only true to their word but competent—or very good at what they do—in order to build trust. Organizational consultants Warren Bennis and Joan Goldsmith (2010) include competence in their definition of *trust* as well, and Jim Knight (2016, 2018), the guru of instructional coaching, identifies competence among his five trust factors based on a significant review of the literature. Drawing from numerous fields, ranging from psychology to philosophy, Tschannen-Moran (2014) cites competence as one of the principal aspects of a framework for establishing trustworthy leadership.

- **Congruity:** Alongside competence, Bennis and Goldsmith (2010) underline the importance of what they call *congruity* in their definition of *trust*— meaning people's words align with their actions. Educational consultant Rebecca A. Frazier (2021) captures this sentiment in her book on effective instructional coaches, explaining that people can claim trustworthiness when they can honestly state, "I can be counted on" (p. vi). Knight (2016, 2018) and Tschannen-Moran (2014), too, allude to this critical trait that equates to one's reliability.

- **Continuity:** When I say *continuity* here, I mean to suggest not only what Bennis and Goldsmith (2010) refer to as *constancy*—leaders demonstrating to staff that they are on their side—but also educational consultant Cathy

A. Toll's (2018) idea that "trust only develops when people are engaged in some sort of activity together" and that "trust develops when two people decide to cooperate in an activity, *particularly when that cooperation occurs repeatedly*" (pp. 14–15, italics added for emphasis). In other words, trust is not tied to a onetime event and might often require remarkable resilience through the ups and downs of a leadership journey. Moreover, "Trust is a reciprocal process: trust begets trust" (Kutsyuruba et al., 2016, p. 347).

o **Compassionate transparency:** Our definition of *trust* would be incomplete if it did not account for a combination of soft skills that allow us to communicate honestly and directly, and with compassion for one another. Combined, these two words, compassion and transparency, delicately balance what so much literature conveys in varying terms, denoting a nonjudgmental and fair assessment of others, among other positive qualities. Leaders are trustworthy when staff believe they are genuinely concerned about others' lives (Bennis & Goldsmith, 2010). In fact, trust is "based on the confidence that the other [person] is *benevolent*," as well as honest and open (Tschannen-Moran, 2014, p. xii). Being compassionately transparent means not only being open and honest but that you are practicing and demonstrating empathy while also assuming positive intentions in those you work with. This generosity of spirit must also involve a level of vulnerability, as Frazier (2021) and Covey (2018) suggest: sharing with colleagues mistakes you have made and explaining what you have learned from them, which in turn allows staff to, over time, feel safe enough to do the same.

This book aligns these essential components, supporting instructional leaders and providing them with practical, actionable guidance on how to establish trust as a foundation in their professional relationships. We all know how it feels when there is no trust, the anxiety and toxicity that consume our thoughts and force us to question everyone around us and even our own ideas. It's palpable, right? Where trust is absent, Knight (2016) reminds us, fear, inertia, and caution reign, but where trust exists, we also find love, joy, learning, and the ability to take healthy risks. In education, trust is everything.

Who This Book Is For

This book is meant to serve as a thought partner for K–12 instructional leaders—one that is solution oriented, with a how-to approach to move beyond the characteristics of trust and offer intentional, practical, reproducible tools for critical trust-building moments in schools. More broadly, this book is for all leaders in education, principals and assistant principals, and those in formal and informal leadership positions; these include, for example, instructional coaches, teachers on special assignment, and resource teachers, as well as teachers who aspire to be in formal leadership positions, all of whom may need or want to develop their individual knowledge and skills to support schools in the implementation of reform (Penuel et al., 2010). In essence, all school leaders are instructional leaders because instruction and learning are, or should be, an educator's central focus. Accordingly, all instructional leaders are tasked to plan, implement, and engage in intentional practices to build trust; yet, as previously mentioned, research that identifies trust and other ideal leadership characteristics, as well as strategies for increasing student achievement, don't always offer the *how* in explicit terms. Instructional leaders need a way to put all this together, including sound advice on what to say—not just do—and *why*. They need a set of protocols they can replicate to guide and coach them. And good coaches know that their coaches need to be able to get what they need when they need it.

The book will be especially useful for aspiring instructional leaders who need practical examples of how to carry out effective protocols, as well as takeaways from leaders in the field who shifted their practices, increased trust, and ultimately bolstered student achievement. Let me provide an overview of the chapters ahead.

Chapter Overview

The book is organized into five chapters, each devoted to one of the five key trust-building practices I have identified for instructional leaders: (1) be visible and approachable; (2) listen closely to the complaint for a request; (3) invite all voices; (4) use a strengths-based approach toward building instructional leadership capacity; and (5) unpack necessary conversations with care.

Chapter 1, "Be Visible and Approachable," focuses on ways for you to be intentionally present as an instructional leader. It offers daily and weekly action items as well as specific questions you can ask teachers and colleagues that also lend themselves to building relationships with students. This initial practice embodies those critical aspects of trust, such as compassionate transparency in the form of empathy, and certainly congruity. Being fully present fosters meaningful dialogue, and through such conversations, you show your genuine interest about others' ideas and tap into productive human interaction (Fullan, 2019; Knight, 2016, 2018). You inspire trust when your best intentions and actions align, or when you both suggest you value visibility and actually make yourself available to staff; in this way, say Frazier (2021) and professor of leadership development Matthew Eriksen (2009), leadership becomes a visible expression of authenticity. Tools for self-assessment are included in this chapter, as well as testimonials from instructional leaders who have experienced challenges related to approachability.

Chapter 2, "Listen Closely to the Complaint for a Request," involves looking beyond staff members' grievances to identify their underlying requests or unfulfilled needs. Here, again, this practice hits on all our components of trust, and it begins with competence in being able to distinguish hearing from the acquired skill of listening. The chapter presents specific activities for you to use with leadership teams to practice various listening skills together—one of which is to go through a collection of common complaints from staff; pinpoint possible underlying requests; and brainstorm next steps, including questions to ask to move the conversation forward. These exercises provide opportunities for instructional leaders to practice listening more actively and thoughtfully for what is really behind a complaint and to also practice posing different types of questions versus engaging in cyclical conversations that often go nowhere. According to Bennis and Goldsmith (2010), Knight (2016), and leadership experts James M. Kouzes and Barry Z. Posner (2017), when staff feel you've listened to them without judgment and believe you actually care about them and their concerns, they know that their work matters and holds significance.

In the same respect, it is imperative for you to think about, practice, and modify how staff receive your messages, particularly with all the different types of modalities available for communication. In this chapter, you'll find listening set-asides to use *before* starting meetings and necessary conversations so that speakers feel valued (Garmston & Wellman, 2016). This list of set-asides is shared in the chapter, along with additional habits to avoid.

Chapter 3, "Invite All Voices," relates directly to continuity and provides self-reflective questions to support your taking an informal inventory of practices currently in place (or perhaps not in place) during various meetings. Protocols and facilitation strategies are included to extend trust by ensuring all voices are welcome and listened to. These explicit protocols help you safely invite all voices to speak up and begin to build a collaborative team where everyone is not only heard but valued, which, according to Michael Fullan and Joanne Quinn (2016a) and educators Parry Graham and William M. Ferriter (2010), moves a group of people from working independently to working interdependently. Indeed, to build precision in pedagogical practices, you must establish an environment that invites and fosters deep collaborative learning for all, and to begin to do that, you must create a safe place for risk tasking, in which each teacher's voice is invited and in which everyone not only is included but *feels* included (Fullan & Quinn, 2016a). In this chapter, instructional leaders share powerful insights after having learned to first examine their own biases or assumptions about teaching and learning, influenced by self-study research methodology (a reflective method to assess our biases), gained pivotal facilitation skills, and let go of the idea that they have to be the experts and know all the answers all the time in order to be leaders (Racines, 2016; Samaras, 2011). Maintaining competence and being an expert are not equivalent (Bennis & Goldsmith, 2010).

Chapter 4, "Use a Strengths-Based Approach Toward Building Instructional Leadership Capacity," walks you through an example of a cycle of continuous improvement that has been successfully implemented at multiple schools across the country and ultimately increased student achievement. The cycle includes an explicit and structured way to build capacity based on strengths, and the chapter further explains *why* this is a critical component in building trust in schools. Each component in this chapter includes self-reflection checklists, instructions for each protocol, and steps for how to implement collaborative learning visits (CLVs) from the ground up. Testimonials from teams are shared alongside what they learned that impacted their work the most and how they *really* felt throughout the cycle of continuous improvement.

Chapter 5, "Unpack Necessary Conversations With Care," focuses on redefining *difficult* conversations as *necessary* ones. You know which conversations these are: the ones you *know* you need to have but you avoid because you don't know where to begin and assume they'll be difficult. This chapter provides specific tools for approaching necessary conversations, as well as a list of mantras that serve as daily reminders for reflection. Authors Robert J. Garmston and Bruce M. Wellman (2016), neurologist Judy Willis (2018), and Knight (2016) explain that for instructional leaders, your mindset matters before you even enter into a conversation.

For instructional leaders, awareness of both verbal and nonverbal communication matters. Peter DeWitt (2022) discusses the importance of communication skills, emphasizing nonverbal communication as equal in importance to oral, written, visual, and electronic communication. DeWitt (2022) stresses the need to pay attention to our body language and facial expressions. Why? Because when we invite people to share their thoughts with us, we must be careful to avoid shutting them down with what we don't say—our body language and facial expressions (DeWitt, 2022). It is as important to be aware of our own and others' body language, as what is said this way—indirectly rather than directly and verbally—conveys a lot of meaning.

Similarly, Irving Seidman (2019) discusses a time when he was interviewing a teacher intern who was describing their teaching in a formal way, yet with super low energy. Seidman (2019) remembers noticing that low energy and, even though the intern was talking positively, the intern's tone and affect was almost too formal, disconnected from emotion. In this case, the verbal communication was not necessarily matching the nonverbal communication. So, Seidman (2019) asked about this seeming lack of connection—and the question opened up a flurry of emotions about what was really going on (how unfairly interns were being treated), which shifted the conversation entirely moving forward so that both the verbal and nonverbal communications matched. Awareness of what is said as well as what is *not* said by both verbal and nonverbal communication is equally important in schools.

This chapter includes a variety of tools and reflective questions to consider before you begin to unpack necessary conversations. I explain different types of questions in great detail to help you reflect, plan, and navigate—from establishing the purpose of the conversation and possible questions to ask and ponder, as Knight (2016) reminds us, to identifying the conversation's ideal outcome for both you and the other person. Reflective questions are shared for before, during, and after a necessary conversation to support you throughout each stage.

Note that you can read this book straight through *or* choose which chapter you would most benefit from without having to go in a specific order. Each chapter includes anecdotes, supporting research, practical strategies or exercises, specific goals, practice scenarios and analysis, reflection questions, and a checklist of action steps. In addition, throughout the book, you will find Virtual Learning Lightbulbs that bring attention to ways to adapt trust-building ideas to hybrid- or distance-learning scenarios. The Educator Spotlights in the appendix at the close of the book offer real-world synthesis of each chapter's content in the form of firsthand accounts of educators who can attest to the utility of the trust-building practice. Collectively, the tools in this book will help you build and often *re*build a strong foundation of trust among instructional leaders and faculty and staff in schools. Finally, I'll remind you to go slow to go fast throughout each chapter as you discover your strengths and needs.

Embark on This Trust Journey

As this book reiterates, you cannot simply tell someone, "Just trust me," and have it magically happen. There are various protocols to choose from to increase student achievement; however, instructional leaders who serve in various leadership positions need actionable advice alongside best practices. You need guidance—a coach—to support your thinking while you take steps. According to educator and leadership coach Peter DeWitt (2015), a mentor or a coach is the most valuable learning asset an instructional leader can have.

While instructional strategies, research, and data have been critical components of all my professional roles in education, I consistently find that earning and maintaining trust is the absolute *core* of each relationship. Trust is what allows for deep, meaningful conversations that mediate thinking, shift practice, and improve teaching effectiveness and learning. No matter which chapter you choose to begin with, by the end of this book, you will know where *you* need to begin and why, and you will have more than a handful of implementable options for both what to do and what to say.

It is worth mentioning, of course, that I, too, have experienced both supportive and toxic work environments, yet I choose positivity every time. I have more than seventeen years of experience as a teacher, award-winning instructional coach, consultant, published author, assistant principal, and principal and have served in every grade level, preK–12, throughout public schools. I've also worked as a professor in both public and private universities supporting educators on both coasts, in Washington, DC and Los Angeles, California. I have effectively transitioned department chairs to instructional coaches through the five key trust-building practices I identify in this book.

Given all these experiences that I am extremely grateful for, I choose and continue to focus on what worked. I choose to focus on listening for requests in others' complaints and assuming positive intentions in every single person I work with and for. I choose to serve as a source of positive change. I kindly challenge you to implement these strategies and share them with the educators you work so hard with each and every day. I am confident that you will experience the same benefits that the educators in this book did to improve relationships within the walls of our most precious institution for teaching and learning: our schools. I ask you, too, to first honor where you are, and next, share your experiences and learning throughout this book. I am excited to embark on this journey with you. Are you ready? Let's go!

CHAPTER 1

Be Visible and Approachable

A school principal's actions in multiple contexts throughout the school matter significantly, no matter how effective a leader this person is from behind a desk. When I took on the role of instructional coach at a new school, I knew that my actions and the extent of my actions—not to mention any inaction—mattered too. Both principals and instructional coaches have an influence on school culture. All behaviors, both the formal behaviors within a structured context, such as while presenting at an assembly, meeting for an evaluation, or coaching a session, and the informal ones, such as walking to and from class, attending a meeting, an impromptu office visit from a colleague, or one of those everyday moments when conversations may or may not happen—all of these behaviors matter for those in instructional leadership positions.

As an instructional coach at a new school, what advice did I receive from Mr. Jones, my new principal?

"Be visible," he said. "Make sure they see you!"

Despite his own advice to be visible, teachers referred to Mr. Jones as "the invisible principal" even when he *was* visible because he often seemed distracted—meaning, even actions can betray a lack of interest. People can tell when a leader simply does not care. However, I discovered that Mr. Jones was actually a terrific listener in one-to-one conversations, and I learned many things from him. However, I also observed patterns of behavior that were counterproductive and the basis for why faculty and staff referred to him as "the invisible principal." He had solid relationships with a few employees, but he hardly stepped out of his office. And when he did leave his office to interact with staff, if someone had a complaint, he would consistently ask them to send him an email with at least three solutions to offer about whatever issue they wanted to discuss. Cringeworthy, right?

Mr. Jones's simply being visible at lunch and telling teachers to email him when they had solutions did not create a foundation of trust. Mr. Jones had a tendency to do a lap around the lunchroom, scrolling through his phone as he walked. He was not present. Staff members often brought concerns to his attention, and in return, he gave a lack of attention to what they were saying. Being visible is different from being present and approachable, and simply telling a teacher to "email me with solutions" not only was cringeworthy but also was rude and dismissive. At times, quick decisions must be made. Teachers look to various leaders to guide them in these moments. Being dismissed under the guise of being asked to take ownership for a concern precludes any chance at garnering any trust. Yet, being visible is common advice for leaders (DeWitt, 2015; Maxwell, 2010; Neumerski, 2013). They often hear: "Make sure they see you." It's not that being visible isn't good advice—it's just that being visible is not enough. As an instructional leader, you must be visible *and* approachable, which means you must be accessible and ready to engage in meaningful conversations. It is also important to note that, if it's not a good time to engage in a lengthier conversation, you must at least acknowledge the importance of a needed conversation. Visibility and approachability are essential as you start to build relationships and garner trust. In this chapter, let's dive into the why and the how for becoming authentically approachable and intentionally present while building a strong foundation of trust, one conversation at a time.

Why Be Visible *and* Approachable?

In his book *Deep Change Leadership*, author and educational consultant Douglas Reeves (2021) reminds us that human behavior precedes belief, meaning that we have to see something before we actually believe it; we have to see that a change is actually working before we offer any real buy-in. When you're an instructional leader, people need to know that you have *constancy*—that you are genuinely going to have their backs (Bennis & Goldsmith, 2010).

According to researchers Aparna Joshi, Mila B. Lazarova, and Hui Liao (2009), if there is a lack of trust or even of shared perception of trust for any of a number of reasons, it often leads team members to lose sight of their common goals and interests and to instead focus on their personal interests. "In these situations," researchers Bart A. de Jong, Kurt T. Dirks, and Nicole Gillespie (2016) explain, "team members are more likely to engage in defensive actions aimed at protecting themselves" (p. 1136). Defensive actions include, for example, complete avoidance and perhaps even condescending comments made with an "I'll show you!" approach. Such behaviors do not move the team forward. The way people react is based on how they feel about *why* there is a lack of trust, and these feelings can result in withdrawal, revenge, and confrontation (Tschannen-Moran, 2014). If you take note of any of this behavior or language among staff, know that it takes time to build, and sometimes rebuild, trust. Be patient with yourself and remember not everything is broken. Look at the school and consider what *is* working well, and then engage in conversations with staff to learn all about them and their concerns.

People need to know that you have constancy, and that includes consistent caring and genuine curiosity about all the things that have been successful and unsuccessful prior to your arrival. Looking back before you look forward is important work in schools. Ask questions when you are approached with concerns, to better understand the entire picture, why it matters, and what else may have happened in the past. There is always a lot of history behind a concern; however, without approachability, you might not ever have some of these very helpful conversations and stories from different perspectives that could otherwise shift your next steps significantly. Gathering background information provides a framework with purpose and guidance before you take any actionable steps. Consider where this advice on visibility stems from and why it matters. Recommendations for instructional leadership have often been broad or vague and, according to educational researcher Christine M. Neumerski (2013), tend to include three key items: (1) identify and articulate your vision and set goals; (2) have a plan to visit classrooms to assess instructional practices; and (3) have visible presence. However, between the three, specific information on *how* to establish visible presence, as well as why it is important, has been largely nonexistent (Neumerski, 2013).

Despite the abundance of evidence linking strong instructional leadership to school achievement and outcomes (Finnigan & Daly, 2017; Forsyth et al., 2011; Rensch, 2019; Saphier, 2018; Tschannen-Moran, 2014), guidance about what *all* instructional leaders should do as instructional leaders has not been necessarily clear, and visibility in and of itself is missing a key component: the importance of direct and personal conversations that take place *during* that visibility (Neumerski et al., 2018). In their study of leadership practices of effective rural superintendents, Mark Forner, Louann Bierlein-Palmer, and Patricia Reeves (2012) offer the thoughts of one superintendent, who articulates that a clear purpose for maintaining visibility is to get direct input to improve schools, particularly to improve student achievement. He suggests having direct, personal, face-to-face conversations when you have the greatest proximity to faculty and staff to talk about ways to improve student learning rather than focusing solely on discipline or administrative tasks (Forner et al., 2012). When you're visible, use accessibility to your advantage; get input and practice listening, because it is in those interactions in which you listen that you create an atmosphere of safety. Remember: teachers must not only *be* included but also *feel* included—and it is when people feel safe and heard that trust begins to be garnered (Fullan & Quinn, 2016a; Wieczorek & Manard, 2018).

Instructional leaders are seen as the carriers of values and can have a positive effect on student learning. However, studies also suggest that, in many schools, instructional leaders don't use their instructional time productively (DeWitt, 2015; May, Huff, & Goldring, 2012). *How* you enact leadership is relevant. Forner and colleagues (2012) examine the literature on leadership practices that support direct, personal conversations and again identify the focus of these conversations to shift toward student learning. Being present, visible, and approachable paves the way for invaluable dialogue that also demonstrates you are interested in others' ideas regarding what's working well and what isn't (Fullan, 2019; Knight, 2016, 2018). If maximized, this time results in a more proactive approach in leadership versus a reactive one.

High school teacher Larry Ferlazzo (2018) interviewed leaders who exclaimed that trust building "happened on my feet, not in my seat," and that the result of these daily interactions were strong relationships. Each interaction becomes a shared experience. It is in these moments, when the conversation stays focused on what is best for all students, that real relationships are built and collaboration is strengthened (Ferlazzo, 2018).

How Do I Lead While Being Visible and Approachable?

So, where do you begin? It's important to assess what you are already doing well in these two categories to then be able to identify where to focus. While of course you can always follow up and ask trusted colleagues about their observations of how you're doing, ask yourself *first*. Remember, this is a starting point that may introduce opportunities for deeper dialogues. When people begin to trust what you are doing, writes Denisa R. Superville (2019) in *Education Week*, the conversations and productivity will be greater as well.

See figure 1.1 (page 14) for a sample self-assessment for determining visibility and approachability. (See page 25 for a reproducible version of this figure.)

This self-assessment helps you reflect on and identify your habits regarding when and where you are visible and perhaps how you could be more visible throughout a typical school day. This assessment further is intended to raise your awareness of what you are thinking about throughout those specific moments that you indicated, and with minor tweaks, can help you align more approachable intentions with your actions.

VIRTUAL LEARNING LIGHTBULB

Visibility and approachability are equally important during hybrid and distance learning. So how can you be more intentional about both? Consider trying these suggestions.

Optional virtual lunch hour with your teachers: This protected time in, for instance, a monthly virtual pop-up lunch hour (as we did at one of my previous schools) is a way to stay connected with teachers in a context outside of academics and instruction. Play games, share what you did over the weekend, or just laugh. There isn't a need to set norms, aside from popping in when you want and staying as long as you want.

Pets-with-the-principal time: Any pet lovers out there? As a principal or an assistant principal, try offering pets-with-the-principal time. Students and faculty can log in and introduce their pets to one another. During the pandemic, I recorded the upcoming school announcements with my beloved dog, Guillermo Felipe, every Sunday at noon. Each video was no longer than five minutes, and I recorded them with a ring-light stand and a cell phone. Traffic increased significantly on our school's Facebook page.

Don't forget one of the most basic expectations for distance learning: having your video on. Many educators lean toward being cognizant of and respecting each student's living situation, but turning off cameras can be a concern. The essence of the frustration comes back to connectivity, not just visibility. Having cameras on is not just about seeing; it's about engagement and about being able to gauge students' understanding nonverbally, too. How do we show up when it comes to video chats? If we expect students to have their cameras on, then what are our own expectations as and for educators?

While visibility does offer a tool for connection and engagement, it is important to acknowledge that Zoom fatigue is real. Géraldine Fauville and her team of researchers (2021) at Stanford University identify specific tips to help educators balance the need to connect through visibility on Zoom with the need to not become exhausted with Zoom use (Ofgang, 2021). Fauville and her team (2021) created a Zoom Exhaustion and Fatigue Scale (ZEF Scale) to identify the causes of Zoom fatigue, and they offer tips to avoid exhaustion, for example, taking frequent breaks and inviting more physical engagement. Fauville and her team (2021) also ask educators to allow students to turn the video off for time-limited periods throughout the lesson, particularly during components that do not require video to be on (Ofgang, 2021). Alyson Klein (2021) similarly addresses Zoom fatigue on behalf of teachers and students identifying headaches as a common symptom of Zoom fatigue. Klein (2021) interviewed Lisa Guernsey, a strategic advisor with the Education Policy Program at New America, and Michael Levine, senior vice president for Noggin, Nickelodeon's online interactive learning service. Guernsey and Levine similarly suggest that it is not solely the amount of time spent in front of the screen that influences how exhausting Zoom use is, but that we should consider the 3 C's: content, context, and the individual child. Instead of asking, "How do we get off screens?" the questions shift toward how to maximize screen time with more engagement. Communication on what makes for valuable engagement is key here, however, and comes back to what is best for the last C: the individual child.

Goal: Align Your Actions With Your Best Intentions

As mentioned previously, we inspire trust when our actions align with our best intentions (Eriksen, 2009; Frazier, 2021). You might intend to be approachable and visible, but then you might find yourself unprepared to engage in a certain topic, which could catch you off guard, leading you to react hastily or in a way that suggests you're getting defensive or trying to avoid the conversation. So, how do you ensure your actions align with your best intentions in this case?

Reflect:

Briefly describe specific times throughout your day when you are routinely visible.

I'm visible in front of the school in the morning, on the playground or blacktop at lunch, walking the halls during bells, in the lounge to greet teachers at lunch, and at the end of the day.

What are you doing? Who is around? Who are you talking to, and what are you talking about, typically?

I'm greeting parents, teachers, students; talking to colleagues, usually about how they are doing or answering questions; or redirecting students' behavior.

Assess:

How might you rate yourself overall in terms of approachability—that is, whether you are accessible and positively engaging in conversations—during the times you've indicated? Mark an *X* on the line.

——————————————————— *X* ———————————————————

| Not approachable | Sort of approachable | Very approachable |
| (Please don't talk to me) | (More focused on task) | (Open and engaging) |

How might your faculty rate you? Mark an *X* on the line.

———————————————————————————————— *X* ——————

| Not approachable | Sort of approachable | Very approachable |
| (Please don't talk to me) | (More focused on task) | (Open and engaging) |

Plan:

Write down specific times during the day when you want to increase your visibility. Why are these useful times to increase your visibility?

Lunch time on the blacktop when teachers go to lunch. During mid-morning break because all teachers are on the blacktop and rotating throughout their grade level. Best time to address questions or things on their mind and check in with them and their teams; pulse check with individual teachers. At the end of the day, I could plan on having my door open or go walk the halls intentionally to say hi to teachers.

What comes to mind for you as you reflect on your day?

I'm not engaged enough. I have too many things in my head, and I'm not focused on the people. I wonder how I'm coming across to various people? I am usually super focused on the task at hand; however, maybe I don't need to be as focused on the task?

Try This:

Look back at your plan and how you rated yourself. Rank the ideas that follow from 1 to 5 in order of the urgency in which you think you need to put them into action.

_2_ Check your mindset *before* you step out of your office. What assumptions do you have about the interactions you might have? Readjust and assume positive intentions.

_4_ Block off various times on your calendar to be among different teachers to invest in more engaging conversations.

_3_ Be intentional about consistently engaging with different staff—maybe keep track of whom you haven't touched base with each week or jot a note to remind yourself to do so.

_5_ Identify days and times to conduct classroom visits at least once a week for informal visits.

_1_ Revamp the type of input you are asking for during your interactions by employing open-ended questions.

Of the questions that follow, which you might ask staff during your interactions, circle the ones that are most useful to you.

- If you could change one thing about this school, what might it be?
- What do you think this school needs instructionally? What do other educators in the school think it needs?
- What is one instructional practice or lesson you would like for me to see?
- (•) I wonder what teachers are passionate about. What are you most passionate about? What about the rest of my staff?
- Tell me about the student you consider your favorite of all the ones you've had.
- What piece of advice would you have for a new teacher here?
- (•) Which year was your best year teaching, and why?
- (•) What is one piece of advice you have for me to be successful here?

Accountability:

How will you hold yourself accountable to being more visible and approachable?

When I arrive to work, I will remember to check my assumptions and mindset before I leave my office for the morning by putting up a sign next to my door that says "Assume positive intentions". This will physically help me remember, every day.

FIGURE 1.1: Determine whether you are visible and approachable.

Try This: Be Grateful, Breathe, and Be Transparent

Be grateful for questions. Even though it might not feel like a gift (leaders are often bombarded with questions), it is positive. You are a leader, and people come to you for guidance. Sometimes people apologize for "having so many questions." Stop the cycle of negativity and apologizing. Thank this person for asking the question.

If you need to, take a deep breath and check your initial reaction. You don't need to answer the question right away, especially if you were caught off guard. Be transparent. You can ask, "Is it OK if I get back to you with a more detailed answer later this week?" or "I might need to think about this a little bit more." You want to do your homework and make sure you have all the most accurate information before you answer. As educators, we consciously provide intentional wait time and encourage students to take a moment to think critically about questions we are asking, and this is imperative when teaching language learners who may need time to mentally translate. We should extend the same opportunities for wait time to ourselves and our fellow adult educators. Providing time to think is critical to teaching, learning, and leading. Be transparent about needing time to consider an answer and give yourself permission not to feel rushed. However, it will be key to schedule a follow-up, and make sure you actually follow up.

Try This: Walk the Talk, and Talk the Walk

It is helpful to be transparent about why you are doing what you are doing. For example, to be more transparent and visit multiple classrooms a week, you should first explain the why and the what behind your formal or informal classroom visits *before* you actually go. Formal classroom visits are certainly dependent upon your position and your district policies; however, for purposes of this example, include evaluative, observation-type visits in the designation of *formal*, as well as scheduled visits from a superintendent or school board members that have a very formal feel to them. Informal classroom visits can be a brief walk-through to see what students are working on and to simply greet students and teachers. All the information about what forms you are filling out (if any), what you are looking for, who you will be paying attention to, and how long you might stop by for is helpful and, of course, depends on your role as well. See figures 1.2, 1.3, and 1.4 (page 18) for examples of a handout and forms that can be shared with teachers regarding the purpose of classroom visits, what might happen during a classroom visit, and feedback. (See pages 27–29 for reproducible versions of figures 1.3 and 1.4.) As most districts have standardized forms for classroom observations, these are intended to clarify the general purpose and procedures for classroom visits. Traditional or more formal classroom visits for observation purposes tend to be silent and create a lot of anxiety. There is room to shift how your daily actions are interpreted by explaining your *why* and *what* beforehand to lower the affective filter of everyone your visit may impact, including classroom teachers and instructional aides. Talk the walk as much as you walk the talk.

School year: 2022–2023

No matter who is observing your classroom (administrator, district personnel, instructional coach, counselor), the mutual understanding and purpose of all classroom visits are to improve teaching and learning. The focus of classroom visits is to focus on school goals (for example, engagement and rigor) through reflection and refinement of practice. There are different roles with different responsibilities, yet the overall purpose of classroom visits is to support teachers and students to improve on our school goals with a strengths-based approach regarding what is working well with our students.

- **Types of visits as administrators:** As administrators, there are two types of classroom visits: (1) formal and (2) informal. Both are intended to provide specific feedback about your strengths, objective observations related to our school goals, and areas to improve, as well as questions that invite your clarification.

- **Types of visits as instructional coaches:** Instructional coaches are *not* evaluators. Classroom visits are intended to focus on a specific teaching method or to improve student engagement using mutually agreed-on data. Coaching conversations are focused on mutually agreed-on goals.

- **A word about collaborative learning visits:** Collaborative learning visits are practiced here at this school. Coaches and administrators participate in collaborative learning visits, which are also categorized as informal classroom visits between teachers. They are intended to build capacity based on the instructional strengths of our teachers.

FIGURE 1.2: Outline of purpose of classroom visit.

*Visit **go.SolutionTree.com/leadership** for a free reproducible version of this figure.*

School year: 2022–2023

The purpose of this form is to not only provide a description about the school as a whole and what to expect in terms of formal and informal observations and classroom visits in relationship to the different roles various leaders play, but also provide these descriptions in writing with the whys behind them, explaining the talk and the walk. It is also important to provide these explanations in writing to provide time to think about these policies, invite room to talk about them, and also be able to refer to them again at a later time.

- **Physical proximity:** Based on the activity of your lesson for the day, the visitor may sit in the back to be less disruptive or may also walk around. The visitor may also speak to students in order to clarify what task they might be working on, with the intention of gauging their growing understanding.

- **Visit length:** Classroom visits are generally around twenty minutes and can happen at the beginning, middle, or end of a lesson. A more formal lesson observation may have different expectations based on the district's agreed-on memo of understanding.

- **Writing:** Some visitors may choose to take notes during your visit instead of writing afterward. Please look at the following half-sheet form that is used for informal classroom visits. Evidence-based statements will be shared—for example, "I noticed" instead of "I liked." One copy will be given to you and placed in your mailbox after the informal visit to ensure transparency and invite conversation after your visit, if desired.

FIGURE 1.3: What's happening during classroom visits. continued →

Teacher: Barbara Stellar

Date: January 15, 2023

Name of visitor: Dr. Racines

School focus: Writing, specifically the graphic organizers used to organize writing and vocabulary used.

Evidence-based student learning (type of data gathered—time on task, questions answered, type of task): Type of task

Evidence-based teacher methods or strategies to highlight (type of data gathered— open or closed questions, strategy or method, opportunities to respond, specific school goals): Strategies used and terminology used that are similar across the TK-8 with regard to the writing process (specific school goal).

Questions and clarifications I am curious about: What is on the wall? Are these what students are producing in teams during the writing process? What step in the process do they represent?

Thank you for having me in!

School year: 2022–2023

Thank you for having us visit. There is a mutual understanding that classroom visits can be uncomfortable and create anxiety. Our intention is to lower that anxiety with the understanding that we are a supportive community.

After forms are reviewed, please feel free to share your feedback, and add anything you wish we would have seen, as that is very common. Please also feel free to invite us back in! Please consider informal classroom visits always in the draft form. Suggestions and feedback are always welcome to the process or forms.

Reflection on Classroom Visit and the Process

1. What is one thing you might do differently based on feedback from this classroom visit?

   I think it might be helpful to ask students to reiterate the writing process step we are working on for the day. I also forgot to ask students to repeat the objective for the day! That step would have helped us both.

2. Might you have any feedback for your classroom visitors or anything you wish we knew?

   I wish you would have known that I was absent the day before. I feel like I was a bit discombobulated and could not find my clicker, which threw me off. I also wish you knew how far my students have come this year, especially given all of our obstacles. They are doing great and have learned so much.

FIGURE 1.4: Follow-up and reflection after classroom visit.

Try This: If You See an Effective Practice, Share It!

Instructional leaders tend to have a broad view of amazing instructional strategies, lessons, and aha moments. However, what good are these moments if they are not shared with faculty and staff? How do others know the extent of your visibility and engagement, and, more important, how will others benefit from the amazing instructional practices going on around campus? Instructional leaders can share what they see in a variety of ways to make sure they engage the rest of the staff with what is going on around campus. As instructional leaders, we—the principal, assistant principal, digital learning coach, counselor, and me—each contributed to a weekly newsletter in Google Drawings where everyone had a "corner," or a column. At the school where we had our Regal Eagle Hour, I called this newsletter *Eagle Eye* and often included links to pictures of instructional strategies as well (see figure 1.5, page 20). I have also seen many similar weekly newsletters created using a variety of online resources (such as Smore, Google Sites, and Constant Contact).

At our school, we would take turns highlighting lessons we saw or student samples of work and explain what strategy was used, along with what grade level and a snapshot of the materials. This was a great way to showcase what each person was exceling at each week in a weekly shout-out. Some weeks, it was focused on the school, and I would include a picture of a project or an example of classroom setup that aligned with the school goals. It was also an opportunity to share open slots for working with the instructional coach or upcoming events.

Goal: Engage the Students to Focus on Teaching Practices

Instructional leaders interact mostly with teachers and other adults. Opportunities to engage with teachers and students, and better yet, students and teachers together, are important for an instructional leader, especially when the focus is on student learning. Identifying classroom ambassadors is a great practice to include to do both and a less threatening way to intentionally increase your visibility and approachability with authentic engagement in the classroom.

Try This: Identify a Classroom Ambassador

Visiting classrooms informally should lean toward engagement versus walking in and walking out. One teaching practice to focus on is being clear about content and language objectives for lessons. While it is important for the teacher, it is more important for student learning. Why? Well, because you know what the most common answer is when you ask students during a classroom visit what they are learning, right? "I don't know!" So, introduce classroom ambassadors. Depending on your school mascot, you can rename it accordingly (Gladiator Ambassadors, Eagle Ambassadors, or so on), and you can start it by piloting it with a few teachers and students who volunteer first.

EAGLE EYE

PRINCIPAL'S MESSAGE

Good morning, Eagles!

Thank you for such a strong implementation of our new intervention schedule! Super smooth transitions and focused on the kids! Way to go!

FROM THE INSTRUCTIONAL COACH

This week, we enjoyed our rounds of collaborative learning visits both at our school and at our neighboring district! One of the requests from our teachers was to see what electives are offered so we can offer more and also see how International Baccalaureate Middle Years Program, and Science, Technology, Engineering, and Mathematics are aligned better. Collaborative learning visits allow for interdistrict collaboration and sharing of best practices!

Want to visit a teacher to learn a new strategy? Join us for our next round of collaborative learning visits. I have two spots left! Thank you!

TECH TIP OF THE WEEK

Do you need to freshen up your strategies, yet you don't have much time to prep? Look no further! Have you tried the website Wordwall? Tons of templates for games that are easy to make! Check it out!

OUR WEEKLY SHOUT-OUT

Have you seen the awesome writing process with reproducible graphic organizers for each step in Mrs. Stellar's class? Of course you haven't; you're busy teaching! Click this link here to go to her class! Want to see how students work through the process? Please contact our amazing instructional coach for a collaborative learning visit! Have an excellent week!

FIGURE 1.5: Eagle Eye newsletter.

If the piloting period is successful and with various shared examples, every classroom is invited to identify an ambassador. The teacher is responsible for choosing ambassadors and back-up ambassadors, and they should rotate, based on the preference of the teacher and taking student grade and ability into consideration.

Ambassadors are intended to serve as opportunities for you to engage with students as a visitor to a class; that way, when outside visitors come by, they, too, can engage instead of simply be visible and observe. This opportunity teaches students social skills to greet classroom visitors and detail what their class is working on. It puts some of the ownership about what teachers are teaching on the students, providing instructional leaders with an opportunity to engage with students about instruction *and* offering students leadership opportunities that their teachers get to observe, celebrate, and enjoy.

VIRTUAL LEARNING LIGHTBULB

The classroom ambassador practice also works incredibly well when visiting classrooms virtually. When I entered virtual classrooms as principal, students were pretty excited to see me and paused what they were doing, welcomed me, and described what they were doing in that moment. Teachers were able to celebrate students' social skills, tech skills, and clear articulation of content and language objectives. If they were in the middle of a presentation, classroom ambassadors often welcomed me in the chat instead of interrupting.

Try This: How Do Students Know How They Are Learning?

Find out how students like to learn. Send out a quick survey or simply talk to the students when you see them both in and out of the classroom. Oftentimes, students are not aware of the intentional teaching strategies and methods implemented. Ask for their views on what is helpful. Are sentence frames helpful? What do they like about the Socratic method? Why do they prefer Pear Deck or Edpuzzle over the other? Ask students to rate certain practices to engage them to talk about various teaching practices and also encourage them to practice the same when they give presentations. This can easily be done over a virtual setting as well with a quick poll in Google Meet or using Mentimeter, so students can see how they all responded.

Goal: Share Announcements in a Variety of Modalities

Being visible and approachable is also applicable to how information is shared through various modalities, including social media. In this digital age, it is important for information to be shared a number of times and in a variety of ways. You truly can't share information enough or in enough ways because individuals have preferences for how they receive information.

Try This: Send Weekly Shout-Outs via Email

Try embedding a shout-out in your weekly announcements or emails to highlight an employee for all good reasons. Upon making this a regular feature, you might find that more people actually read the announcements because they want to know who received a shout-out! You can support colleagues with so many acts of kindness that might otherwise go unnoticed. This practice also connects employees to one another, particularly people new to the school.

Try This: Make Video Announcements on Your School's Facebook Page

The weekly shout-outs described in the preceding activity might also be mentioned in weekly video announcements. I recorded video announcements with my dog with a ring light and a cell phone, and they were always less than five minutes long. They would include meetings and events that were coming up and weekly shout-outs. (Staff loved them and, of course, were amazed at all the dog costumes for each holiday—see figure 1.6). Video announcements are a great way to stay connected, answer any questions, and simply have a little bit of fun sharing good news.

FIGURE 1.6: Video announcements.

Try This: Use the Remind App

Last, but not least, there are several apps to help you deliver information directly to smartphones. The Remind app has become such a popular tool to use, and it can also translate to multiple languages. Visit www.remind.com for more information about using this tool.

Remember to keep information short and sweet (for example, if picture day is around the corner, simply state, "Reminder for Eagle Elementary School: Picture Day is on 5/15!"). In text form, it is best not to send lengthy reminders; it's only a reminder. I also recommend identifying the name of the school in the message, as parents may have students in multiple schools.

No matter which of the aforementioned methods you choose to use, remember that each one is an extension of ways you stay visible, connected, engaged, and approachable. Remember that everyone takes information in differently. Do not get frustrated when people say they didn't get the information you shared. Instead, ask them how they prefer to get the information, and use the experience as an opportunity to engage. Your efforts go a very long way and do not go unnoticed.

School Scenario

Barbara is an elementary school teacher who piloted an initiative identifying classroom ambassadors in her fifth-grade class before the rest of the school. The student chosen to be the classroom ambassador was very nervous, and he completely blanked out the first time he was called upon to be ambassador, at which point the observing assistant principal guided him to where he was supposed to look for the classroom objectives so that he was able to remember them.

The assistant principal's gentle guidance reminded Barbara of the purpose of classroom ambassadors: for students to reflect on what *they* are learning, and she and the assistant principal met afterward to discuss ways educators support this purpose. The goal of the program was not just about entering the classroom and being greeted by the classroom ambassador. Ambassadors provide a way for all to get to know one another better.

Through these interactions, Barbara and the assistant principal were able to build a stronger relationship; Barbara was able to express her vulnerability about her insecurities in trying something new that did not go perfectly. Change, however, happens one conversation at a time, and over time, with small adjustments made, the class got the hang of it and soon began inviting the assistant principal to come back more often so they could practice sharing what they were learning. It was fun and provided an opportunity for the assistant principal to be visible and approachable with both the teacher and the students.

Conclusion

Visibility and approachability are key for building trust. However, the results of meaningful interactions are most important. Having a plan to be more present builds strong relationships. Remember your *why* as you foster these dialogues.

See the applicable **Educator Spotlights** in the appendix at the end of this book (page 113) for examples of how real educators took risks, employed trust-building practices, and fostered collaborative communities to bring genuine visibility and approachability to their work.

Your goal is to learn more about ways to improve the school; why not learn that directly from your teachers through conversations? Fostering opportunities for valuable dialogue provides a distinct method for being proactive about solutions, versus being reactive about problems. Remember, an environment that fosters deep collaborative learning for all must be in place to build precision in pedagogical practices founded in the creation of a safe place for risk tasking. The following reflection questions and action steps help you begin to do just this.

REFLECTION QUESTIONS

Review and record your responses to the reflection questions so you can refer back to them periodically and track your progress in building trust.

1. What will you do to be more visible and approachable?
2. When you consider your current daily or weekly schedule, is it more aligned toward being proactive or being reactive?
3. What are you curious about regarding your school and teachers? Engage teachers in conversations about these topics.
4. If you are not in a virtual- or hybrid-learning environment, could you incorporate at your school some of the online ideas mentioned in this chapter? Which ones?

A CHECKLIST OF ACTION STEPS

Check off each of the following items as you complete it.

☐ My self-assessment includes the Plan section of figure 1.1 (page 14).

☐ I have blocked off items on my calendar to remind myself to do them.

☐ The strategy I will use to hold myself accountable toward implementation is _____.

☐ I will reassess my level of engagement again on _____.

Determine Whether You Are Visible and Approachable

Reflect:

Briefly describe specific times throughout your day when you are routinely visible.

_____

_____

_____

_____

What are you doing? Who is around? Who are you talking to, and what are you talking about, typically?

_____

_____

_____

_____

Assess:

How might you rate yourself overall in terms of approachability—that is, whether you are accessible and positively engaging in conversations—during the times you've indicated? Mark an _X_ on the line.

_____

Not approachable   Sort of approachable   Very approachable
(Please don't talk to me)   (More focused on task)   (Open and engaging)

How might your faculty rate you? Mark an _X_ on the line.

_____

Not approachable   Sort of approachable   Very approachable
(Please don't talk to me)   (More focused on task)   (Open and engaging)

Plan:

Write down specific times during the day when you want to increase your visibility. Why are these useful times to increase your visibility?

_____

_____

_____

_____

What comes to mind for you as you reflect on your day?

_____

_____

_____

_____

Try This:

Look back at your plan and how you rated yourself. Rank the ideas that follow from 1 to 5 in order of the urgency with which you think you need to put them into action.

_____ Check your mindset before you step out of your office. What assumptions do you have about the interactions you might have? Readjust and assume positive intentions.

_____ Block off various times on your calendar to be among different teachers to invest in more engaging conversations.

_____ Be intentional about consistently engaging with different staff—maybe keep track of whom you haven't touched base with each week or jot a note to remind yourself to do so.

_____ Identify days and times to conduct classroom visits at least once a week for informal visits.

_____ Revamp the type of input you are asking for during your interactions by employing open-ended questions.

Of the questions that follow, which you might ask staff during your interactions, circle the ones that are most useful to you.

- If you could change one thing about this school, what might it be?
- What do you think this school needs instructionally?
- What is one instructional practice or lesson you would like for me to see?
- What are you most passionate about?
- Tell me about the student you consider your favorite of all the ones you've had.
- What piece of advice would you have for a new teacher here?
- Which year was your best year teaching, and why?
- What is one piece of advice you have for me to be successful here?

Accountability:

How will you hold yourself accountable to being more visible and approachable?

_____

_____

_____

_____

_____

Trust as the Core of Instructional Leadership • © 2022 Solution Tree Press • SolutionTree.com
Visit **go.SolutionTree.com/leadership** to download this free reproducible.

What's Happening During Classroom Visits

School year: _____

The purpose of this form is to not only provide a description about the school as a whole and what to expect in terms of formal and informal observations and classroom visits in relationship to the different roles various leaders play, but also provide these descriptions in writing with the whys behind them, explaining the talk and the walk. It is also important to provide these explanations in writing to provide time to think about these policies, invite room to talk about them, and be able to refer to them again at a later time.

- **Physical proximity:** Based on the activity of your lesson for the day, the visitor may sit in the back to be less disruptive or may also walk around. The visitor may speak to students in order to clarify what task they might be working on, with the intention of gauging their growing understanding.

- **Visit length:** Classroom visits are generally around twenty minutes and can happen at the beginning, middle, or end of a lesson. A more formal lesson observation may have different expectations based on the district's agreed-on memo of understanding.

- **Writing:** Some visitors may choose to take notes during your visit instead of writing afterward. Please look at the following half-sheet form that is used for informal classroom visits. Evidence-based statements will be shared—for example, "I noticed" instead of "I liked." One copy will be given to you and placed in your mailbox after the informal visit to ensure transparency and invite conversation after your visit, if desired.

Teacher: _____ Date: _____

Name of visitor: _____

School focus: _____

_____

_____

_____

_____

_____

_____

_____

_____

_____

Evidence-based student learning (type of data gathered—time on task, questions answered, type of task): _____

_____

_____

_____

_____

_____

_____

Evidence-based teacher methods or strategies to highlight (type of data gathered— open or closed questions, strategy or method, opportunities to respond, specific school goals): _____

_____

_____

_____

_____

_____

_____

_____

Questions and clarifications I am curious about: _____

_____

_____

_____

_____

_____

_____

Thank you for having me in!

Follow-Up and Reflection After Classroom Visit

School year: _____

Thank you for having us visit. There is a mutual understanding that classroom visits can be uncomfortable and create anxiety. Our intention is to lower that anxiety with the understanding that we are a supportive community.

After forms are reviewed, please feel free to share your feedback, and add anything you wish we would have seen, as that is very common. Please also feel free to invite us back in! Please consider informal classroom visits always in the draft form, and suggestions and feedback are always welcome to the process or forms.

Reflection on Classroom Visit and the Process

1. What is one thing you might do differently based on feedback from this classroom visit?

_____

_____

_____

_____

_____

_____

_____

_____

_____

2. Might you have any feedback for your classroom visitors or anything you wish we knew?

_____

_____

_____

_____

_____

_____

_____

_____

_____

CHAPTER 2

Listen Closely to the Complaint for a Request

'll be honest: when I used to hear someone complain in meetings, I was taken aback. I felt uncomfortable. I remember attending our quarterly department meeting my first year as a new teacher. The meeting had not yet started, but teachers walked into the room and immediately started complaining to one of the civics teachers, Mr. Bryan, also the Student Council Association adviser, about an email that Mr. Bryan had just sent out to the whole school. The email stated the date and time for the talent show. Apparently, it was scheduled for the same day as the final civics test. Mr. Bryan and another history teacher on the team, Mrs. Stohr, got into a heated argument, and I vividly remember Mrs. Stohr exclaiming to Mr. Bryan, "Just forget it, because unless it's English or mathematics, administration really doesn't care anyway." I didn't know exactly what to do or say.

I always remember this interaction between Mr. Bryan and Mrs. Stohr, and although most complaints don't usually get quite as heated as this one did, regardless of how a complaint reaches you as an instructional leader, it is usually filled with emotion and has a historical context of some sort, and there is always a request (or two) in there somewhere. I've mentioned the importance of looking back before you look forward before, and it is important to recognize why this is so important here as well. The school was functioning before you arrived; it has a past, and this is all the more reason to be open, listen deeply to the complaint for the underlying requests, and invite others to do the talking to learn about these previous experiences. I always find that each unique conversation adds one more piece that I did not know, oftentimes about the interpersonal relationships at the site, that enriches the context to my overall understanding of the history of the school. It was a few years later that I learned, as author and workshop facilitator Dave Ellis (2002) advocates, "to listen for the request in a complaint" (p. 183), and when I play back this conversation, I hear it differently. Jim Knight, Jennifer Ryschon Knight, and Clinton Carlson (2017) emphasize this point under the four elements of being a good listener. A lot was said in the interaction between Mr. Bryan and Mrs. Stohr, some of it without actually being verbalized, but the key message was: civics was not a priority. This wasn't the first time that large school events were calendared without input from this department, and staff felt no one really cared, so why bother?

I no longer hear complaints; I hear requests. I listen differently. My only regret is not learning this skill earlier in my career, because it shifted how I communicate and improved my craft of teaching and learning significantly—with teachers, parents, *and* students. Like author and civil rights leader Valarie Kaur (2020), I learned that "the most critical part of listening is asking *what is at stake* for the other person. I try to understand what matters to them, not what I think matters" (pp. 143–144). *Listen to the complaint for the request* has become my daily mantra, so much so that I had it printed. I keep it posted where I can read it before I begin my work for the day.

Before we jump into the work, pause and think about the last complaint you received. Where were you? Who was speaking to you? What was it about? How did you feel? What was your initial reaction? What did you say? What did you not say? Was it resolved?

This chapter outlines the why and how for shifting from hearing complaints to listening closely to the complaint for a request, with strategies to try in various scenarios with different educational partners. Learning to listen is harder than it sounds (pun definitely intended).

Why Listen Closely to the Complaint for a Request?

Educational consultant Shelly M. Arneson (2015) shares that teachers refer to communication as the greatest trust builder. However, as instructional leaders, we often falsely assume that successful communication rests on the content of what we say (Bennis & Goldsmith, 2010). Author Susan Cain (2012) walks us through a number of perceptions we have of leadership: we see talkers as leaders and regard them as being smart, which we often equate with having power. Cain (2012) states that the more a person talks, the more group members direct their attention to that person, meaning the speaker becomes increasingly authoritative as a meeting continues. Moreover, we tend to rate quick talkers as more capable and appealing than slow talkers. However, there is no correlation between more talk and greater insight; we actually tend to overestimate how outgoing and talkative leaders really need to be (Cain, 2012). Instead, writes professor of organizational behavior Erik van de Loo (2016), *listening*—one of the most basic human activities—is "one of the most important determining factors for the quality of interpersonal and professional relationships" (p. 121).

Changing how you listen and what you listen for is transformative because it changes how you go about understanding people. It seems to be a forgotten, and unfortunately overlooked, skill. However, and again, it's another skill leaders are often encouraged to simply get better at. The harsh truth is that most of us do not actually listen very well at all (Knight, 2018). If we take a hard look at our own daily activities, it should come as no surprise that, according to Libby V. Morris (2014), Zell B. Miller Distinguished

Professor of Higher Education at the University of Georgia, listening has declined given the host of social media and educational practices: texting, tweeting, and participating in asynchronous online instruction. Platforms that elevate visual over auditory (minus music) and abbreviated written communication dominate our communication habits (Morris, 2014). This is not to say that there is no value in those forms of expression—there is! Listening, however, is critical for engaging in more meaningful communication, particularly listening to the complaint for the request, and it neither is quite as instinctive as it seems nor develops naturally. According to professors of educational leadership Douglas Fisher and Nancy Frey (2019), president of Adelphi University Christine M. Riordan (2014), Cain (2012), Knight (2017), and van de Loo (2016), listening must be explicitly developed—and it begins with an understanding of the distinction between hearing and listening.

Educators Suzanne F. Peregoy and Owen F. Boyle (2017) explain that of the four language domains of (1) listening, (2) speaking, (3) reading, and (4) writing, listening is often coupled with reading, and together they are referred to as receptive or passive skills. Writing and speaking are considered productive or active skills because they require some sort of language output. It is hearing, however, that is a passive component *of* listening. Listening is active. We listen for meaning, with the end result being interpretation of meaning—what we think the information we heard means. Listening requires effort, because according to Willis (2018), if you are truly listening to someone, you are tuning in, refraining from judging, validating the person you are listening to, offering nonverbal responses, asking questions, and acknowledging or even restating what the other person says. Knight (2016) contends that questions are the *yang* to complete the *yin* of listening. If we *don't* ask questions, we limit our opportunities to listen, and if we do not listen, our questions do not have a purpose (Knight, 2016).

It is specifically these mental processes that need to be fostered in both teachers and students (Fisher & Frey, 2019; van de Loo, 2016). Why? Because they create a safe environment. Van de Loo (2016) explains that our capacity to understand that behavior—the effort to make sense of what is being said—is influenced by unconscious responses and by things that we cannot physically see, including feelings, fears, and hopes. It is influenced by unobservable states of mind. *Mentalizing* is how we make inferences about people and their behaviors (van de Loo, 2016). Mentalizing effectively often means listening, asking questions, and clarifying understanding about what we hear. Together, these practices help create a safe environment that is focused on a collective effort to understand one another.

Journalist Kate Murphy (2020) emphasizes that choosing to not listen at all or to continue to listen poorly, without trying to improve, only deprives you of becoming the best version of yourself as a more trustworthy instructional leader, and it ultimately limits your understanding of the world. Those who listen closely and carefully to others are not only receiving information but also trying to make sense of what is being said, particularly when the information is a complaint (van de Loo, 2016). In their daily face-to-face conversations, instructional leaders often need to act swiftly in response to complaints. Yet even in those circumstances, it is important that they truly *listen* to first identify what staff are really requesting under that complaint, rather than immediately offer to solve the explicit, surface-level problem—because what appears to be the issue in the moment is not always the root issue. In those moments, too, depending on your relationship with your teachers, you might hear what educator Irving Seidman (2019) refers to as people's *inner voice* or *outer voice*—meaning they are actually telling you what they honestly mean (inner voice) or they are using guarded words and cautiously crafting their language as if speaking to an audience (outer voice). This is yet another reason why actively listening and asking probing questions are imperative when it comes to grasping what is *really* meant (Seidman, 2019). See table 2.1 for examples of inner-voice comments alongside their outer-voice counterparts.

TABLE 2.1: Inner Voice Versus Outer Voice

Inner Voice	Outer Voice
"My day-to-day is terrible. None of us get along on my team. We argue every single day, and none of our conversations are productive."	"My day-to-day work with my team—let's just say . . . it's an adventure."
"Friday's deadline is *not* realistic. You know that, right? What happens if we run out of time? Do we *all* still have to do *all* of it?"	"How might I ask you this to be politically correct—are you expecting us to be finished with *all* district assessments by Friday?"

Murphy (2020) shares that out of all the interviews she conducts for her articles, the most memorable are ones in which the interviewees veer off unexpectedly into more personal stories, often disclosing information that they've never told anyone else. Murphy (2020) believes it is because she listens so closely that individuals feel able to entrust her with their stories; that listening in and of itself creates the opportunity for such special, unfiltered moments. And research certainly substantiates this. According to Knight (2017), Kouzes and Posner (2017), and Riordan (2014), both active listening and caring about what people say, or showing empathy, communicate respect and allow people to share information, which creates an environment centered on trust. As Kaur (2020) argues, to inhabit another person's view of the world—to have empathy—is to feel the world with that person. Active listening is a powerful skill for achieving this level of connection and assurance in a relationship.

Before we look at tips and strategies for how to listen, and especially at how to listen to the complaint for the request, I want you to first reflect on when and how you learned to listen. For instance, did your school or classroom have stations where you put on headphones to listen to a story and then answered questions based on what you heard? I find it interesting that models of listening demands are infused into instruction, particularly listening stations for students. For example, Judi Brownell (2018), a professional of organizational communication, identifies six key components of active listening in her HURIER model.

1. Hearing (registering the sound)
2. Understanding (decoding the spoken message)
3. Remembering (storing and retrieving the message in memory)
4. Interpreting (intoning, making facial expressions, and offering visuals)
5. Evaluating (listening critically or assessing the message)
6. Responding (listening interactively or taking action)

However, according to Fisher and Frey (2019), adults hardly practice these despite the increasing availability of podcasts, digitized radio broadcasts, audiobooks, and the like. There is no doubt that effective listening takes time and practice. The results, however— trustworthy relationships—are worth every ounce of effort. People trust us when they know we truly care about them, and we can show them we care by listening and internalizing what is at stake for *them* (Kaur, 2020).

How Do I Listen Closely to the Complaint for a Request?

Where do you get started? Think about your school. Using figure 2.1 as a sample and the reproducible template from page 46, list the top five complaints you hear. These complaints can be from anyone who is part of your school.

1.	I have no idea where we are supposed to meet. Like, online? In a room? where? I just won't go!
2.	Do you really expect us to pass these common assessments? We are nowhere near that content yet! Just letting you know.
3.	what a horrible day. with my luck, I should have expected tech not to work, my lesson to go south, and student behavior to be at its worst during my observation.
4.	Everyone in my department does their own thing. There is no community of learners here. Maybe on paper, but not in real life.
5.	How am I supposed to teach these high-level math concepts to this group? They are so far behind; it's impossible.

FIGURE 2.1: Top five complaints in your school.

Now reread the top five. Star the top complaint you've recorded and use figure 2.2 to help you or your leadership team determine the underlying need or request in the complaint. (See page 47 for a reproducible version of this figure.)

Goal: Improve How You Listen—Small Shifts to Practice Daily

If you want to improve something, you can't wish your way to that improvement. You have to *practice* every day, making small shifts that add up over time. This incremental development applies to being a better listener; and by better, I mean a genuinely engaged and interested listener, someone truly curious about how people are feeling and thinking about the topic of conversation. Why should we care about improving to try to be a more engaged, more interested listener? Because, as Knight (2016) reminds us, everyone experiences greater well-being when they are engaged and heard; ultimately, in this way, we build trust. Similar to the advice we give teachers in learning a new instructional strategy, and who, in turn, teach it to students, we explain it, we model it, and then we possibly have a coach support you or model it with you. To improve at something, we need time to practice it and further reflect on how the shifts we make are making a difference. The following Try This sections are intended to invite this practice and reflection through the introduction of new strategies, explanation of how to do them and why, and the identification of time to try them and further reflect on your takeaways.

Try This: Validate, Validate, Validate!

Sometimes during a conversation, especially when someone is complaining, there is often a misunderstanding due to miscommunication. Problems develop when what we hear and think we understand does not match what someone says and means. Not only do listener interpretations sometimes not match intent, sometimes what people say isn't actually what they mean. Among the common barriers in communication, as Knight (2016) emphasizes, are the perceptual errors that we all make that interfere with receiving and sending a clear message. When we do not understand something, we find a way to explain that confusion away (Knight, 2016). Sometimes, it is our own explanation that mixes up the message even further. Another common response to these situations is to simply continue the conversation without pausing to ask for clarification. If you are really trying to actively listen, it is good practice to clarify meaning whether you suspect you are encountering a miscommunication or not. Paraphrasing is a helpful strategy to validate meaning, and it takes practice (Costa & Garmston, 2016). The most important thing is to make sure you are clear about what speakers mean, whether you paraphrase or ask a clarifying question. In terms of the latter, one of the best questions I have ever learned to ask is what author and thought leader in coaching Michael Bungay Stanier (2016) shortens to *AWE*, that is, the practice of asking, "And what else?" Three magical

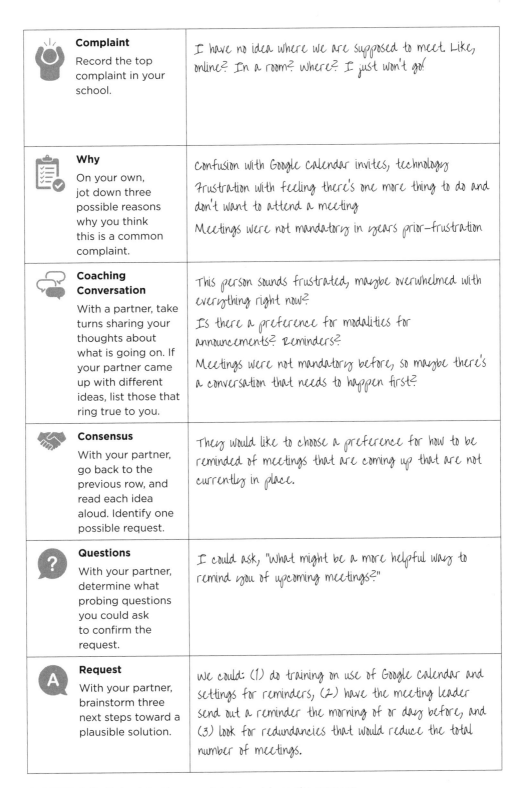

	Complaint Record the top complaint in your school.	I have no idea where we are supposed to meet. Like, online? In a room? Where? I just won't go!
	Why On your own, jot down three possible reasons why you think this is a common complaint.	Confusion with Google Calendar invites, technology Frustration with feeling there's one more thing to do and don't want to attend a meeting Meetings were not mandatory in years prior—frustration
	Coaching Conversation With a partner, take turns sharing your thoughts about what is going on. If your partner came up with different ideas, list those that ring true to you.	This person sounds frustrated, maybe overwhelmed with everything right now? Is there a preference for modalities for announcements? Reminders? Meetings were not mandatory before, so maybe there's a conversation that needs to happen first?
	Consensus With your partner, go back to the previous row, and read each idea aloud. Identify one possible request.	They would like to choose a preference for how to be reminded of meetings that are coming up that are not currently in place.
	Questions With your partner, determine what probing questions you could ask to confirm the request.	I could ask, "What might be a more helpful way to remind you of upcoming meetings?"
	Request With your partner, brainstorm three next steps toward a plausible solution.	We could: (1) do training on use of Google Calendar and settings for reminders, (2) have the meeting leader send out a reminder the morning of or day before, and (3) look for redundancies that would reduce the total number of meetings.

FIGURE 2.2: Delve into the complaint to address the request.

words put together to form a question will provide you with even further insight and details than if this question went unasked! See table 2.2 for more examples of what to say to gain clarity on a speaker's concerns.

TABLE 2.2: Responses for Gaining Clarity on Staff Concerns

Staff Concern	Paraphrased Reply	Clarifying Question or Questions	Next Step
"How am I supposed to get my students ready for the district assessment next week? I'm three weeks behind! There's absolutely *no* way. I can't do this. They are all going to fail."	"You're feeling a bit anxious and defeated and do not feel like your students will have covered all the material before the test."	"And what else?" (Stanier, 2016). Ask this question after their response to your paraphrased reply, because more might be going on than what they vocalized initially before you paraphrased.	"Out of all the standards you have to cover, what might be the key standards to review before the assessment?" "Let's look at a calendar over the next three weeks and plan backward with the key standards you have identified in mind."

Try This: Don't Resist Resistance

In your agenda, if you are asking for input about how to improve something and are clear about that as a desired outcome, be prepared for an array of ideas that you might not agree with and that not everyone will agree on. Maybe the entire group feels that action is not necessary and that what you are proposing is not a priority. Do not resist that resistance—remember, you asked for input! Seek common ground versus common dividers in this resistance (Knight, 2016). As an instructional leader, you will meet resistance to many things. Don't shy away from it. Expect it. Let the resistance serve as data points for you. Change is often hard! Instead of avoiding it, acknowledge it, and, further, aim to understand it. Why is there resistance? Approach the resistance with a lens of clarification first. (Figure 2.2, page 37, may be used to help you distinguish what is driving the resistance and further identify how to support a shift toward plausible, mutual solutions.)

Try This: Flip That Phone Over

You've been there before. You're talking to someone, sharing something you consider incredibly important, and then you notice *that glance*—the glance that the other person takes at his, her, or their cell phone (or smartwatch). In fact, many of us are guilty of doing this. But when we divert our eyes to look at our devices, we make the other person feel less valued (Frazier, 2021). This action does not go unnoticed, and it communicates to the other person that we are not listening; we've checked out of the conversation. We lose trust in these moments because we not only seem disengaged but in fact *are* disengaged. Authentic listening is something we feel as much as we see (Knight, 2017). If we really care about what others have to say, we should be fully present in our conversations, and refraining from checking our devices is one habit that demonstrates we respect those with whom we're speaking (Knight, 2016).

Goal: Make Objectives and Outcomes Clear for All Agendas for Every Meeting

One way to address complaints is to prevent them by being more detailed and explicit in explaining the purpose of agenda items in meetings, specifically in identifying the rationale behind specific line items and their relationship to schoolwide solutions. Meetings could include monthly faculty meetings, various schoolwide committee meetings, and subject or grade-level teams. One of the top complaints I hear from teachers is, "What is *this* meeting going to be about?" followed up with, "Why are we doing this?" How many staff meetings have you sat through without really knowing either the purpose of the meeting or the expected outcome? Have you ever attended a meeting in which the leader rushed to finish or get through all the agenda items, allowing no time for questions and therefore leaving participants with more questions than answers? I certainly have! Oftentimes, this is not the leader's intent, which is all the more reason to be deliberate when it comes to planning.

Try This: Create an Agenda

Listening as an instructional leader comes in many forms, and how you structure and set up your meetings is one of them. One of my highest recommendations for instructional leaders is to craft a straightforward agenda, with clear desired outcomes for every item on the agenda, and carve out time to listen to everyone. If you are new to a site, it's worthwhile to share how you prefer to communicate to each of your educational partners, which could include, depending on your role, faculty, staff, and parents, and leave space for feedback about the format you prefer to use. Explain how this format sets the tone for honoring each person's time, delineating purpose, and always reading over the agenda to welcome suggestions or additions *before* you begin. I recommend sending out the agenda and asking for feedback, changes, or suggestions to it at least one week in advance. I often would send in a Google Doc with the "comments only" privacy setting activated so I could see multiple suggestions and the reasoning behind each suggestion. It's helpful. This does not mean you have to change your entire agenda after receiving feedback; it means you acknowledge what is important to everyone and try to find a time to address it, if possible.

Take note of the facilitator: Are groups hearing from the same instructional leader each time? It is helpful for teachers and staff to hear from different instructional leaders at meetings. Encourage new or aspiring leaders to facilitate a meeting with your support. Are there opportunities for other instructional leaders to share in a leadership opportunity to facilitate a portion of the meeting? Think about using these agendas as evidence of the frequency of shared leadership opportunities as well.

See figure 2.3 for a sample agenda for meetings based on meeting agendas developed by consultant Ann Delehant. (See page 48 for a reproducible version of this figure.)

Agenda Item	Desired Outcomes	Facilitators	Estimated Time	Next Steps and Due Dates
Welcome and Introductions	Introduce ourselves to the collective group.	Principal	5 minutes	Take note of any absences to make sure to include at our next meeting.
Norms and Today's Meeting Outcome	Select two or three cocreated norms to focus on given the focus of today's meeting, which is to go through data from last year's state assessment broken down by English learner (EL) proficiency levels, and identify three areas of school focus.	Assistant Principal	5 minutes	Revisit the norms at each meeting to align the meeting objectives with the norms.
Data Dialogue Process	Identify what is in each grade-level folder, and read through the entire protocol together to work through data to identify areas of strength and improvement.	Coach	20 minutes	Reiterate the identified strengths and areas of improvement to the entire faculty to confirm school focus areas by 9/30.
Reflect and Connect	Identify our thoughts about today's meeting and any new connections we are making toward our larger school community and our process (1 sticky note for each).	Coach	5 minutes	

Source: © 2009 by Ann Delehant. Used with permission.

FIGURE 2.3: Agenda for meetings.

Why is setting a clear agenda important overall, and how does doing so garner trust? There are two reasons why it is valuable: first, it shows transparency in what we are doing, for how long, and why, and second, if you value and honor people's time, and want to show that you honor it, then respect it. Start and end meetings on time. If you run out of time, do not just keep going—find a space to close the meeting and ask to meet again at a future date. Or, if *all* teachers would prefer to finish the work, get permission to do so from the *entire* team. Some team members might have other commitments. Don't blame them for that. For every meeting, it's essential for you to state clear objectives and desired outcomes and to allow time for questions. If you say you care about others' input, and if you follow up by distributing an agenda that will allow them to gather thoughts and questions they'll have time to express, then your words match your actions and you're building trust (Bennis & Goldsmith, 2010).

Try This: Unfinished Business? Jot It Down!

I encourage instructional leaders, before they start a meeting or conversation, to jot down the things they are thinking about that they will need to get back to after their meeting so it doesn't distract them *during* the meeting. This strategy is helpful as you begin to practice listening more actively. It is also very easy to get off task during a meeting, especially if someone brings up a new question or a new task unrelated to the current topic, so jot it down and mention that you are making a note to discuss at length later. If you go into a meeting with this strategy in mind, it will help you set aside things you are thinking about or that naturally come up that will distract you from being a more effective listener throughout your entire meeting or conversation.

Goal: Remember, Aim to Coach, Not Consult

According to educators Arthur L. Costa and Robert J. Garmston (2016), teachers report far more satisfaction with coaching than with consulting. Your end goal as an instructional leader is to build capacity, which includes nurturing the self-efficacy and ownership of your teachers' solutions, not necessarily your own. So, ask yourself *how* you are listening to your teachers: Are you listening to solve or to understand? And furthermore, are you listening to ultimately help your teachers solve their own problems without you? While both coaching and consulting are intended to help others solve problems, if you are listening only to solve, you are consulting more than you are coaching. Costa and Garmston (2016) delineate specific differences between consulting and coaching, specifically in conversations; for example, a consultant might state, "Here are ways to approach this" (p. 13), whereas a coach would instead ask, "What might be some ways to approach this?" (p. 13). Peter Block emphasizes that a coach shares their perspective but does not own a specific idea or action that results from the coaching process, whereas a consultant "does have *some* influence over a specific change or action taken by an individual or organization" (as cited in Bloom, Castagna, Moir, & Warren, 2005, p. 80). Listening as a coach can be extremely beneficial and builds strong relationships and trust.

Try This: Explore Their Solutions Before Offering Your Own

When your teachers come to you and voice their concerns about the pacing guide or another district assessment due date, or when they are extremely stressed out about their lessons for their evaluations, listen and *ask clarifying questions first.* When you instead provide immediate, plausible solutions, you foster a sense of dependency and set a precedent, inviting that practice to continue (Costa & Garmston, 2016). What you permit, you promote, right? Your concerned staff must have taught multiple successful lessons in the past, even as student teachers, so what did they do then? Ask them to walk you through *those* lessons. Similarly, a complaint about a pacing guide is often a request for time, and it begs for support with backward planning to identify what lessons staff do in fact have time left for. Such concerns often stem from teachers' anxiety about not having covered certain concepts and their feeling judged because their scores will be lower as a consequence. I often hear, "Who wrote this assessment? I haven't covered any stuff like this!" Shift the focus; ask what staff can do (or have done in the past), and have them offer their own solutions first. It is tempting to jump in at this point and try to solve their problems, but here you must trust that, while you may be addressing a concern in the short term, you may not be getting to the root of the issue. Take the time to listen and provide this meaningful support that will pay dividends for your whole team.

Try This: Practice Listening

As suggested throughout this chapter, listening is a skill that we all must intentionally practice. Figure 2.4 outlines two listening protocols to help you practice listening with a partner within your leadership team. Note that the protocols are intended to help you practice listening more actively and are not intended to mimic how you listen in a natural conversation. While listening is a technical skill, the objective here is not for you to practice constricted listening; instead, it's about focusing on what to listen for as you become more cognizant of what the other person is saying, as well as developing and expressing genuine curiosity and empathy. These protocols are like those used in conflict resolution with students, where you allow time for each person to share. It will become more natural over time. No matter what position you are in, every coach needs a coach to practice listening skills.

Try This: Ensure Your Speaker Takes Center Stage

Before you begin a conversation, it's often worth considering: are you *really* ready to listen? A few things you can do is to practice listening set-asides, as referred to by Garmston and Wellman (2016). Let's take an example of when you hear a conversation regarding a celebration of a successful moment. Try not to jump in with a "Me too!" statement. Resist the temptation to share your similar experience in that moment (Racines, 2019). It may be well intended, but you may go off on a tangent about your experience. In this way, though perhaps inadvertently, you fail to honor the other person through listening, and you detract

Sample Listening Protocol 1

Coach the Coach: Listening Duos

Think about current problems you are experiencing in your school. List out a few. Circle the one that you could use the most support with. Once you each have your problem, remind yourselves to help each other stick with the directions for each step of the protocol. Try not to deviate in conversation away from each step. Practice listening in duos using the following prompts. Each action should last two minutes.

1. The first person explains their current concern at school.

2. The second person validates what the first person stated.

3. The first person explains what has been tried individually or what they have in mind to address this concern and the result of any attempts as well. Also add what efforts have been tried both schoolwide and districtwide, if applicable.

4. The second person asks questions to help the first person consider additional plausible solutions or next steps.

5. The first person shares new ideas for next steps, as well as which one they will try first and why.

Partners may now switch roles. The time for each step is approximately 2 minutes.

Sample Listening Protocol 2

Coaching the Coach: How Well Did You Listen?

You can either ask yourself these questions or interview your partner using these questions.

- What did you notice about yourself during protocol 1? Circle the following item that best reflects your listening.

    I hardly listened   I still need to practice a bit   I'm an effective listener

- Where did you want to move away from the protocol or feel the need to interject?

- Do you find yourself listening differently now?

- What is something your partner noticed about you during protocol 1?

- What is one thing you need to work on for next time?

FIGURE 2.4: Listening protocols.

*Visit **go.SolutionTree.com/leadership** for a free reproducible version of this figure.*

from their experience and excitement (Racines, 2019). So, what do you do instead? Take the opportunity to learn more about what made this such a positive experience. Set aside sharing your experience for a later time. The following list offers some examples for what to say instead to ensure the focus remains on your speaker.

- "Wow, this is amazing! Tell me more about this."

- "This sounds really interesting! How did your students like it?"

- "I'm so excited for you for trying something new!"

- "I can't wait to see this in action sometime!"

- "Are you open to teaching us all how to do this sometime?"

> ## VIRTUAL LEARNING LIGHTBULB
>
> If you must quickly flip to virtual learning, remember that it will be important to keep your team united. Losing physical contact with people is difficult. Add a sticky note to your laptop to remind yourself to open meetings by asking participants to share good things to celebrate. What are some of your small wins or celebrations to share out? This will reinforce keeping your teachers and their collective wins at center stage.

School Scenario

My aha moment as an instructional coach actually came unexpectedly. I was taking a self-study research course in which I was using this methodology to examine how my own experiences as an English learner influenced my effectiveness as an EL instructional coach to ultimately improve my practice and increase student achievement (Racines, 2016). It was during an interview where I was actively listening to one interviewee and she said to me that she did not have any experience teaching ELs at all, while my other interviewee, who had been raised as an EL, told me she felt she couldn't share her experiences because they were "only" her experiences as an EL.

Really listening to both teachers raised my awareness in that moment, and instead of listening to either as a complaint, particularly as a complaint about ELs, I listened for the request in their concerns and realized that one teacher was begging for help and the other teacher had all the valuable insight to help ELs and simply wasn't trusting herself. I was cognizant of my own experiences as an EL, while also validating the experiences or lack of experiences of teachers, and I recognized a need to balance my own assumptions to build relationships and honor all teachers, no matter their level of experience. This increased my effectiveness as a coach. My listening for others' requests improved their practices and mine, and we all objectively recognized what educators Hugh Munby and Tom Russell (1994) refer to as *the authority of our life experiences*. Had I heard, or interpreted, only a lack of experience, it would have been a lost opportunity for me to help improve teaching and learning for all of us.

See the applicable **Educator Spotlights** in the appendix at the end of this book (page 115) for examples of how real educators' learning to listen had a positive impact on their work.

Conclusion

A shift from hearing complaints to listening to the complaint for the request is transformative because it changes how you go about understanding your faculty. This in turn helps you support their personal development and growth in areas where they need help and ultimately improves teaching and learning for students. When teachers feel you have listened to them with positive intentions and judgment suspended, trust increases because they know you care about them and that you value their work (Knight, 2017; Kouzes & Posner, 2017; Riordan, 2014). Distinct from hearing, actively listening with empathy encourages people to share their inner voices and freely exchange ideas, and it can shift a school environment in a more positive direction that's positively palpable (Seidman, 2019). The following reflection questions and action steps provide support in developing trust-based listening practices.

REFLECTION QUESTIONS

Review and record your responses to the reflection questions so you can refer back to them periodically and track your progress in building trust.

1. When you consider your current approach toward receiving or hearing complaints, is it more aligned toward offering solutions (consulting) than asking questions (coaching)?
2. What will you pay attention to in yourself the next time someone complains to you?
3. What will you pay attention to in others the next time you are telling a story or hearing a story (versus a complaint)?
4. What rings true to you now about the difference between hearing and listening?
5. Out of all the tips in this chapter, which one will you need to practice the most?

A CHECKLIST OF ACTION STEPS

Check off each of the following items as you complete it.

- ☐ I have identified at least one listening exercise to continue practicing with my team.
- ☐ I have identified at least one listening exercise to continue practicing by myself.
- ☐ The next time a person talks to me, I will try not to interrupt.
- ☐ The strategy I will use to hold myself accountable toward implementing new listening skills is _____.
- ☐ I will reassess my ability to actively listen again on _____.

Top Five Complaints in Your School

1.
2.
3.
4.
5.

Trust as the Core of Instructional Leadership • © 2022 Solution Tree Press • SolutionTree.com
Visit **go.SolutionTree.com/leadership** to download this free reproducible.

Delve Into the Complaint to Address the Request

Complaint Record the top complaint in your school.	
Why On your own, jot down three possible reasons why you think this is a common complaint.	
Coaching Conversation With a partner, take turns sharing your thoughts about what is going on. If your partner came up with different ideas, list those that ring true to you.	
Consensus With your partner, go back to the previous row, and read each idea aloud. Identify one possible request.	
Questions With your partner, determine what probing questions you could ask to confirm the request.	
Request With your partner, brainstorm three next steps toward a plausible solution.	

Agenda for Meetings

Agenda Item	Desired Outcomes	Facilitators	Estimated Time	Next Steps and Due Dates

CHAPTER 3

Invite All Voices

Instructional leaders set the tone of collaboration in schools. Instructional leaders who promote a school culture that emphasizes cooperation and caring rather than competition will more likely have higher levels of trust among teachers (Arneson, 2015; Fullan, 2019; Tschannen-Moran, 2014). Schools must ensure not only that all teachers are heard and included but that all teachers *feel* included (Fullan & Quinn, 2016a; Graham & Ferriter, 2010).

When I was a new assistant principal in a school, I made sure to follow the lead of my principal, as this was a new administrative position for me, having come in as an instructional coach. It is also important to note that the principal was also new to the school, although not the district. So, what did our first few encounters with the faculty and staff look, feel, and sound like? Very nice, actually. Friendly faces and a warm environment. We learned that more than half of this faculty had been teaching at this school (and this school only) for well over twenty years; indeed, they were a tight-knit community. They also knew about the principal from her work elsewhere in the district. What else did we notice? The same people were always volunteering, speaking up, serving as coaches, and helping us both get situated to our new school. Was there anything terrible about this? Not entirely. So, what was wrong with the same group of nice teachers volunteering for everything and speaking up all the time?

The problem wasn't so much that the same people were speaking up. The problem was that the other group of teachers were simultaneously never heard from. As I learned more about the school culture, it became clear that the changes in leadership over the past few years meant that, while a few teachers did speak up a lot because they felt they had to keep the school together, others felt that there was a group of favorites and one of nonfavorites. Those who felt like have-nots explained that they were reprimanded in different ways for not always agreeing with the majority. This revealed a little more about why we did not hear from everyone. This is one example of why it is always so important that instructional leaders look back at the history in a learning community and invite feedback from everyone, including the quieter teachers. It's valuable to find out everyone's perspectives before jumping ahead. Sure, each individual might have a very different account of what happened or why things didn't work out; however, that is the perspective of that teacher and should be honored. That is how they interpreted whatever it is that happened. If you don't uncover all things that happened and how they affected different people while you were not there, you might be missing a lot of details that may be worth considering. You don't know what you don't know. In this instance, we had to ask ourselves, "Are we making any efforts to gain participation from everyone?" And at the time, we weren't.

When I was a coach of coaches in a different district, there was a similar concern related to eliciting participation. Coaches shared that they did not feel comfortable leading certain meetings because they felt they had to be the experts and had to know all the answers. Because of a shift in their positions from teachers to coaches, they feared losing trust or credibility from their colleagues if they did not now know everything, and they did not feel comfortable asking quieter teachers to speak up. Jim Knight (2021) says it best when he says coaches "can and should have expertise—they just shouldn't *act* like experts."

Both schools had different circumstances yet similar issues in eliciting all voices to be heard. What about your school?

This chapter offers explicit structures and protocols that have successfully supported instructional leaders in ensuring everyone has a voice that is listened to and valued. Fullan (2019) encourages this type of surface-level change to be addressed in such a nuanced manner to authentically move a group of people from working independently to working interdependently, and it begins with a review of why this actively inclusive approach is so critical for all instructional leaders (Fullan & Quinn, 2016b; Graham & Ferriter, 2010).

Why Invite All Voices?

Professional speaker and leadership consultant Tim McClure notes a concerning sign of employees feeling unimportant when he says, "The biggest concern for any organization should be when their most passionate people become quiet" (T. McClure, personal communication, January 24, 2022). Knight (2016) recalls a conversation with Gallup Senior Scientist Shane J. Lopez regarding the research he completed with Preety Sidhu that looked at what categories of employees answered "yes" when asked whether people felt their opinions really counted at work. Out of the 150,000 surveys, want to guess what category of employee came in last? Teachers! In all fifty states, more often than construction workers, for example, teachers felt their opinions mattered very little (Knight, 2016). Those in the one profession that makes all other professions possible feel their opinions matter the *least*?

According to Manfred F. R. Kets de Vries, Konstantin Korotov, Elizabeth Florent-Treacy, and Caroline Rook (2016), numerous conscious and unconscious group dynamics influence individual and group effectiveness, how well an organization functions, and overall morale. Group dynamics similarly influence classroom participation among students, say Douglas Fisher, Nancy Frey, and John Hattie (2020), and teachers must utilize a variety of engagement strategies to elicit what students are thinking. But, as educator Melinda Malik (2016) explains, while the notion of participation and group dynamics is similar with adults, adults learn and share their learning differently than students.

The late Malcolm Knowles (as cited in Malik, 2016) asserted the key principles of adult learning theory, or *andragogy*—how adults learn. Malik (2016) reviews these principles in their application to professional development and concludes that adults need real-world application of their knowledge and experience. They need the opportunity to learn in self-directed ways, and they need acknowledgment of their wealth of experiences and opportunities allowed to serve as a resource to others. They need the purpose for their learning to be clear and relevant now (versus the future) in order to consider it valuable.

Most adults are invested in where they work; there's a sense of ownership, and they prefer not to play political games (Kets de Vries et al., 2016). Yet, unfortunately, we often do not actually know what others know, feel, and want unless we intentionally elicit feedback from *all* teachers. What ends up happening, as author John C. Maxwell (2010) explains, is that we make assumptions about what we think *everyone* knows, feels, and wants. Playwright George Bernard Shaw (as cited in Arneson, 2015) captures this common misstep well: "The single biggest problem with communication is the illusion that it has taken place" (p. 57). Everyone has something to offer, everyone's perspective must be acknowledged, and what you say as an instructional leader must connect with what you do, as such congruity builds trust and increases credibility. If you do care about staff's perspectives, you must put in place specific protocols to hear them—*all* of them, especially the quiet ones (Bennis & Goldsmith, 2010; Kouzes & Posner, 2017).

An environment of motivation and mutual respect must be thoughtfully created. To create this type of environment, one in which you can garner trust, you must first *extend* trust. One way to do this is by freely inviting questions, suggestions, and solutions for important daily work (Frazier, 2021; Fullan, 2014; Kets de Vries et al., 2016). Bennis and Goldsmith (2010) call this *participatory empowerment*, where people are authentically empowered to be a part of the decision-making process and feel that they are making small steps of progress in their daily work. Once you establish this type of working environment, you level the playing field, trust increases, and the culture becomes more collaborative; it shifts to a less top-down model (Arneson, 2015).

Instructional leaders should participate as learners with their teachers, yet it is critical to emphasize that it is the process itself—the learning and leading—that's important, a phenomenon that authors Roger L. Martin and Sally R. Osberg (2015) refer to as *expertise and apprenticeship*. That is, to become an expert at what you know, you also have to be open and learn from others about what you do not know, like an apprentice (Martin & Osberg, 2015). Instructional leaders must draw others in and know how to elicit their voices because good teachers, leaders, and speakers do not view their own interests as the most important, and they don't see themselves as the only experts, with passive audiences that they need to impress (Maxwell, 2010). It is the ability to see and act on the behalf of others and have a sense of advocacy and empowerment, where the learning is with the team, and more importantly, the focus is authentically on the team over self (Fullan, 2014). Learning becomes a two-way street (Fullan, 2016). It is then that the school builds trust.

Cain (2012) highlights another reason why it is essential for instructional leaders to include everyone's voice: introverts. Not everyone is an extrovert, and explicit protocols and structures are necessary for us to hear from those who are less inclined to verbalize their thoughts and expertise in certain settings (Cain, 2012).

It takes effort to get to know everyone's strengths and perspectives, especially in a larger group, where introverts are overpowered at times. Cognizant instructional leaders take the time to learn about and listen to all people in the room, making the most of everyone's unique strengths and insights and using the attendant information to build leadership capacity (Fullan, 2014; Maxwell, 2010).

Now, let's walk through why providing specific structures for instructional leaders is so critical and review practical strategies, including self-assessments, to better elicit equitable participation and advocate for ensuring all voices are heard.

How Do I Invite All Voices?

First and foremost, why do instructional leaders need such tailored structures, strategies, and protocols? Political scientist Paul Manna (2015), in a report from the Wallace Foundation, shares that for too many school districts, leadership development is an afterthought and instructional leaders are largely left on their own to rely on their own knowledge and intuition to determine what it means to be an instructional leader, which, as emphasized by Bradley S. Portin and colleagues (2009) and Nona A. Prestine and Barbara Scott Nelson (2005), results in large variation in how they enact the role. Principals' own professional development issues receive limited attention, and any efforts to meet their needs are commonly an afterthought, rather than an important part of the collective solution provided for teachers (Manna, 2015).

Similarly, Manna (2015) notes the pattern of time spent on professional development meetings that tend to focus on describing mandates and new initiatives in an overwhelming regurgitation of information without preparing leaders for how to facilitate the delivery of these new initiatives within their respective schools. It comes as no surprise that the National Association of Secondary School Principals (2020) reports that 42 percent of leaders, specifically principals, indicated that they were considering leaving their position, with the most common reason cited as inadequate access to professional learning opportunities. This also commonly includes teacher leaders, instructional coaches, and assistant principals, who need the skill set to put a stronger focus on learning and the how-to support to get started with practical ideas (DeWitt, 2015).

The idea of what instructional leaders must do and the reality of what goes on at schools each day are disconnected as the day-to-day has shifted significantly away from traditional, more managerial models of leadership and toward a more shared, collaborative leadership approach (Neumerski et al., 2018). Taking to heart the following protocols, strategies, and tips, instructional leaders will be able to invite all individuals to be heard, as well as convey from the outset that every contribution adds value and richness to the conversation. The practical ideas will facilitate a systemic approach to professional development that fosters safe, deep collaboration (Fullan & Quinn, 2016b).

Goal: Ensure an Environment Conducive to Sharing

It is much easier to be able to move forward and make what appears to be collective decisions if you hear from the few teachers in a meeting who participate in a discussion or share an opinion quickly. However, why are we in a rush? What are we racing toward? While the school year does move quickly, it will be more valuable to pause and make a collective effort to include everyone's voice in order to hear *all* perspectives so you can more thoughtfully consider issues that might otherwise have been limited.

Try This: Take Informal Inventory of Current Practices in Meetings

Take a moment to reflect on each of the following statements, which will allow you to consider whether practices currently in place promote equitable participation from everyone on your team.

- I strongly value the opinions of everyone on our team.
- I have a protocol in place that invites everyone's thoughts.
- I have each agenda item delineated with a clear purpose, outcome, and an adequate time frame for consideration.
- I have a set of team-created norms that we utilize.

If you read through this inventory and think to yourself, *I don't have any of these in place*, that's okay—because now it means you are aware of the gap areas where you need to do some work. And, the opposite is also true if you have some of these in place, but perhaps you are inconsistent with them—for example, using norms. It is *very* easy to meet with the same group of people each time and want to skip that step; however, remember that you are modeling good practices, so stay consistent. Find ways to remind yourself or keep it on your agenda to hold yourself accountable for practicing what you preach!

Try This: Review Purpose as a Norm With *Norms*

Reviewing purpose as a norm ensures that each meeting is managed more objectively, and staff's connection to purpose heightens their levels of engagement and productivity (Kets de Vries et al., 2016). When you can make clear to people that their work matters and *how* their work matters, both intrinsic motivation and participation increase (Kouzes & Posner, 2017).

When you encourage others' participation, you signal to them that you welcome their suggestions, and when you make a habit of reviewing your working agreements or goals as a team, you convey that together you will not tolerate interruptions or dysfunctional behaviors, particularly those that serve to silence others (Kets de Vries et al., 2016). I encourage you to cocreate norms with staff so that each member has an opportunity to provide input. Overall, norms support how your team members work and how you invite participation. And when you give team members these opportunities to share knowledge and information, trust will ultimately increase. The following list contains sample norms.

o   Remember that students are at the heart of raising the bar and closing achievement gaps. Be student focused in intent and effort.

o   Follow a purposeful agenda that honors time commitments.

o   Respect one another by actively listening and presuming positive intentions.

o   Come prepared with a learner's lens and respect the learning curve.

o   Invite and honor everyone's perspective.

o   Work toward consensus when making decisions.

o   Speak openly and honestly for the good of the group.

o   Have fun, value humor, and insist on laughing.

o   Actively participate and unplug.

VIRTUAL LEARNING LIGHTBULB

Remember that *netiquette*, or norms for distance learning and online meetings, is just as important to keep intact as norms for in-person meetings. As mentioned previously, it is essential that we look at our own online practices and how we ask for participants to show up for online meetings. Sharing norms or reminders for netiquette guides participants with the expectations for how to show up, it designates purpose, and it can also create a structure for all participants to share their thoughts in an organized manner. Norms can include muting yourself upon entering a virtual meeting room or inviting participants to share which norms they want to focus on by adding their preferences in the chat. As an instructional leader, you must be diligent about maintaining the collaborative environment, indicating that an online meeting doesn't equate to lax norms. Establishing and modeling netiquette will guide your team's work and how you elicit participation.

Try This: Have a Conversation With Your Faculty

During a faculty meeting, share what is important to you and what you envision with your faculty. Things that are important to you are often noticed in your actions; however, people can't commit to what you envision if you do not share it explicitly as well, perhaps then opening a discussion about how actions support vision. While I encourage you to share your vision for your ideal school, do you know what your teachers' visions are for what their ideal school environment looks like? What about your staff? Your administrative team? Have you ever asked? What would their ideal school look like? Feel like? Ask them. Maybe they have never been asked to share what they envision. Provide time for them to do so as a group. You could hand out a sticky note to each person to jot down ideas first and then ask them to share with a partner so you can ask what they want to share or what they heard their partner share as well. Does this mean you will immediately implement everything? No. It does mean that you now know what everyone envisions in an ideal school and what matters to everyone in creating an environment where everyone feels like they are a part of a collective whole.

We tend to ask who else agrees with an idea, but what about encouraging ideas different from our own or ideas that are in the minority in a group? In a group discussion, consider asking those with an idea that is only supported by a minority to shift the conversation by further exploring and expanding on their ideas with the group. Support trying new ideas with encouragement by stating what we are not going to say if a new idea does not work, but instead celebrate trying something new. Ask your faculty about their thoughts on the concept of trying and celebrating new ideas and perhaps on how they think shifting this understanding could impact participation in the classroom.

You want everyone to feel safe to share their thoughts and not feel outnumbered if they don't agree with the majority, so remind people regularly that there's power in having your own unique ideas and, further, in sharing them!

Goal: Lose the Desire to Be an Expert at Everything

Assumptions: We all make them, both about other people as well as about what we as instructional leaders tell ourselves we have to be. When you let go of assumptions, even just a little bit, that powerful learning *can* take place. As instructional leaders, we sometimes assume that we must know all the answers or be the expert at everything, and we also assume that others will judge us if we fall short in either knowledge or expertise. Placing such unrealistic expectations on yourself will distract you from the real work. While instructional leaders *do* need to exhibit competency, that does not equate to being an expert at everything (Bennis & Goldsmith, 2010). But this is not just important for instructional leaders to know; teachers, too, must know this about their leaders, and leaders must communicate this same expectation of teachers—that is, the expectation that no single person has all the answers—along with the added message that working as a team benefits everyone, most especially our students. So, to practice what we preach, we must also extend assuming positive intentions in others as well. This level of transparency creates trust, and the type of environment where there is no judgment increases sharing of ideas. Leaders do, however, need to know how to invite dialogue to be able to elicit different areas of expertise from teachers.

Try This: Rate Yourself

One request that my teachers made to me as an instructional coach was to help figure out who was well versed in what capabilities when it came to our school goals, to better be able to build capacity from within our campus and seek help from one another— a less top-down model. During our professional development meeting, we first charted each of our school focus areas—EL engagement strategies, tech tools, and Common Core State Standards and curriculum alignment—on separate charts. Teachers each had sticky notes to write down what skills, scaffolds, instructional strategies, or teaching methods we had collectively worked on or tried to implement or to develop in each category throughout the year. For example, for tech tools, they included Pear Deck, the interactive presentation tool for Google Slides, or Socrative, the cloud-based student-response system. We then took that list and sorted them as a faculty. We placed duplicates on top of one another, and from there, we asked teachers to rate their expertise using sticky notes once again.

We asked teachers to write their names on a few sticky notes and place their names under *beginner*, *intermediate*, or *advanced* for the top three strategies. For example, Pear Deck was one strategy the entire faculty chose, and we were able to see that half our staff felt they were experts while the other half had not tried it yet, or they considered themselves beginners. See the different examples of this activity in figures 3.1 and 3.2 (page 58). Our intention was to offer more tailored professional development opportunities in the future instead of risking staff sitting through workshops they did not need, and we wanted the group members to further work together to build up their strengths, in essence, what Fullan and Quinn (2016b) suggest as using the group to change the group. Creating a collaborative culture where teachers can learn from one another is one way to include everyone in the process of shifting practice (Fullan & Quinn, 2016b).

VIRTUAL LEARNING LIGHTBULB

You can also conduct the rate-yourself strategy using a Jamboard, an online whiteboard, to elicit the top strategies under each larger category. Jamboard lends itself to sorting through each strategy to identify larger categories and further inviting staff to rate themselves. Google Forms or Padlet can also be used for the rate-yourself strategy as a beginner, intermediate, or advanced learner for each category under each school focus area.

EL Engagement Strategies				
		Beginner	**Intermediate**	**Advanced**
Skills Strategy Method	Say Something	Jackie	Katie Christy	Terry
	Socratic Methods	Sam	Emily Barbara	
	Sentence Frames			Jess Rob Lulu Liz

Tech Tools				
		Beginner	**Intermediate**	**Advanced**
Skills Strategy Method	Pear Deck	Natalie Ian Diego Sylvia Dennis		Aleb Lana Lauren Stephan Dante
	Socrative	Rob	Rose	
	Vocaroo			Lulu

Common Core State Standards and Curriculum Alignment				
		Beginner	**Intermediate**	**Advanced**
Skills Strategy Method	i-Ready		Rachel Joan Barbara	Jess Kathy
	Achieve the Core (https://achievethecore.org)		Tiffany	Kate
	Common Core State Standards Initiative			Kathy Jen

FIGURE 3.1: Example 1 of staff development strategy—Rate yourself!

*Visit **go.SolutionTree.com/leadership** for a free reproducible version of this figure.*

Strategy or Technology Used to Address School Goals	Proficiency Level (Select one.)			If applicable, check this column if you'd be willing to share your expertise.
	Beginner	Intermediate	Advanced	
Say Something			*Tiffany*	✓
Actively Learn	*Lulu*			

FIGURE 3.2: Example 2 of staff development strategy—Rate yourself!

Visit go.SolutionTree.com/leadership for a free reproducible version of this figure.

Try This: Let Go of Assumptions

Most effective leaders want to make a contribution that is larger than themselves (Fullan, 2014). Good leaders also want to learn more, are often humble, and want to offer something to help others (Fullan, 2014). When you move into a new instructional leadership position, there is a need to balance continuously learning and being okay with not knowing everything all the time, and if you're going to assume anything, assume positive intentions in that everyone around you is doing the best they can. Allow yourself to let go of the assumption that you have to know everything, especially in a new role, and instead, shift your understanding of knowing everything to an appreciation for the characteristics of competency as, in part, resourcefulness, knowing where to find the answers if you don't have them (Frazier, 2021).

Maxwell (2010) shares how artist Walter Anderson observed that one of the most difficult risks we take is being honest with ourselves, particularly when we realize that others have knowledge about things we don't. Go into your new role with this mindset as well. Be curious about what knowledge others have. I relate this notion of being okay with not knowing everything to letting your guard down just a bit and simply being comfortable with being yourself. Fullan (2014) suggests using the expertise you do have to make a difference in a way that you can, in the area that you are passionate about and that you are good at, and learning the skills you need to learn in the areas in which you do not yet have expertise.

Goal: Lead With Low Stakes and Ease Into Full Participation by Offering Selections

Inviting everyone's voice takes strategic effort; however, the best way to work toward that goal is to simply start. Ease into full participation by offering selections and figure out what works best for your site.

Try This: Spend an Eagle Buck

Think about the last meeting you had. I am confident you can determine who will identify a mistake you made or the person who always asks a question that was already answered. Yes? However, what if I asked you whether you can identify who typically has a handful of solutions? And how about who will speak up regarding how they feel about those solutions? The intention behind this strategy is to provide an example of a protocol that allows all participants to share their perspectives without judgment as a group works toward making a decision.

For example, at the school where our mascot was the eagle, we adapted Garmston and Wellman's (2016) general spend-a-buck strategy, in which members have imaginary coins they can distribute among predetermined options, calling it *spend an Eagle buck*. After a very lengthy presentation of options for our new intervention block schedule, staff narrowed seven different options down to four but had difficulty deciding on one and only one. From there, both myself, the assistant principal, principal, and resource teacher provided each faculty member four sticky notes, and each of the four options was posted on its own chart around the room in a gallery-walk fashion. Each sticky note represented a quarter of one Eagle buck, and each faculty member was asked to spend the entire Eagle buck. The option for intervention was chosen based on how all participants spent their sticky notes. Each sticky-note value was totaled, and that was how we chose our intervention block. Overall, the process of spending Eagle bucks was fun, and it was an easy way to ensure all staff were included, heard, and accountable for sharing their choices.

Try This: Line It Up—Pros, Cons, and Something New?

One activity we participated in at the beginning of each school year was choosing our three school goals based on our previous year's school data. However, data alone were often not enough to make a collective decision. Similarly, what we each had to let go of was our favorite choice. So, we would participate in a lineup to share pros and cons for *each* school goal we listed as choices. We would line up in two lines and walk up in one direction and share the pros and turn around and then share the cons. This was a really quick way of making sure all ideas were heard from everyone. After each round of lineups, we would ask for volunteers to bring attention to anything they heard that they had not previously considered—something new? There was always a new idea and also something to consider if we were going to use that goal to help us measure it. Of course, this also encouraged everyone to simply talk to one another, and this was often a much needed break to get up, move around, and talk to one another too.

School Scenario

Joanna was a new instructional coach in a school where she had taught for almost three years. Prior to becoming an instructional coach, she was a traditional department chair and had never facilitated any meetings before. During one of our meetings, she shared that trying to help everyone speak up made her really nervous because these teachers are her colleagues and her friends, and she didn't want to put them on the spot to speak up! This assumption came with the fear that her new leadership position involved losing trust or credibility from her colleagues.

It was after her coach modeled the spend-an-Eagle-buck strategy with her that she was able to see that you do not have to embarrass people or single people out in trying to elicit their participation. Joanna had never learned specific facilitation strategies outside of teaching students, so this was exciting, new learning for her.

Conclusion

Learning how to invite everyone's voice shifts the energy in an environment for instructional leaders and teachers and promotes collaboration. When everyone feels important and listened to and believes that their perspective actually matters, it changes how teachers work with one another; everyone's voice is invited, and more important, every voice has value. The following reflection questions and action steps bring attention to the practice of valuing all voices.

See the applicable **Educator Spotlights** in the appendix at the end of this book (page 116); you'll find examples of real educators developing an appreciation of all voices and growing that into inclusion of all voices.

REFLECTION QUESTIONS

Review and record your responses to the reflection questions so you can refer back to them periodically and track your progress in building trust.

1. What practices do you already have in place that intentionally include inviting the voices of all faculty members?

2. What will you pay attention to in others during your next faculty meeting with regard to equitable participation from everyone?

3. What will you pay attention to in yourself?

4. What rings true to you now about why it is so critical to include everyone's perspective?

5. Out of all the strategies in this chapter, which one will you implement right away, and why?

A CHECKLIST OF ACTION STEPS

Check off each of the following items as you complete it.

- ☐ I have identified at least one protocol to practice with my team.

- ☐ I have identified at least one exercise to practice by myself.

- ☐ I will look for ways to include everyone and use a protocol to elicit each person's participation.

- ☐ The strategy I will use to hold myself accountable toward ensuring all voices are heard is _____.

- ☐ I will reassess my progress for eliciting everyone's input throughout the year on a _____ basis and measure that growth by _____ _____.

CHAPTER 4

Use a Strengths-Based Approach Toward Building Instructional Leadership Capacity

The concept of flattened leadership, explains journalist William Craig (2018), is where leaders are on the same hierarchical level as all their teachers—a flat model intentionally structured to promote everyone's participation. Throughout this chapter, I will use Pinewood Lawns Middle School (a pseudonym) as an example of one school's journey to build mutual trust and instructional leadership capacity to ultimately flatten leadership.

Pinewood Lawns is a Title I school that consists of thirty-five teachers and serves more than one thousand students, with approximately 70 percent of the student population identified as having low socioeconomic status. Ninety-two percent of the school is Hispanic, 2 percent is African American, and 6 percent is White. Pinewood Lawns is a three-year public middle school serving students in grades 6–8 and offering services for gifted and talented students in a magnet program, students with learning disabilities, and students who attend English for Speakers of Other Languages (ESOL) classes.

Teachers at Pinewood Lawns were cordial to one another, and while there was no lack of conversation in the teachers' lounge, the talks were rarely about instruction. The talks were about students, and usually not with the best connotations. Yet within each individual classroom, there were dozens of great instructional strategies being executed every single day. There was hardly any collaboration among teachers about teaching and learning. Professional learning communities functioned more like meetings where administrative tasks were discussed in lieu of instruction.

The school also functioned like two separate schools on one physical campus: magnet on one side of campus and non-magnet on the other. Biweekly grade-level team meetings often had brief disagreements that stemmed from the range in ability levels of the students on each team that led to inequitable workloads. Surface-level conversations were amiable and followed a traditional top-down leadership hierarchy. Team morale was consistently low, trust was very low, and teachers mainly worked in silos—in essence, there was no team. Within a school like Pinewood Lawns, where do you begin to build instructional leadership capacity, which is critical to building trust? Why a strengths-based approach, anyway—and what exactly does that mean?

A strengths-based approach focuses on what each teacher brings to the table. What instructional skills are they exceptional at? Maybe it's Socratic circles or maybe it's ease with the use of technology—maybe it's the seamless way they redirect behavior, or maybe it's a project that happens each year that everyone gets excited about. Whatever it is, it's worth highlighting, sharing, and teaching one another, perhaps. Instead of focusing on all the things that are not working in a school (and not to say that there's no attention to what's not working), bring to light the teachers' outstanding skill sets and focus on those strengths that each person brings. There were *so* many untapped skills that I was able to see as an administrator, but teachers are teaching, and they don't get to see all the amazing lessons in action. Think about that teacher and that pure magic that exists when you walk into their room . . . whatever that sounds like or looks like, where students are engaged, noisily or quietly, and taking in all the learning. It's palpable when you walk in, and it puts a smile on your face. Yet when teachers are working in silos, who will ever uncover what is happening in those silos? How would you ever know?

Let's dive into both the *why* and the *how* for taking on this important work.

Why Use a Strengths-Based Approach Toward Building Instructional Leadership Capacity?

According to researchers Robin Martin, Susan O'Hara, Joanne Bookmyer, and Renee Newton (2020), there is an urgency to meet new standards, accountability requirements, and ambitious teaching goals, and teachers need systemic and ongoing opportunities for collaborative professional learning. However, traditional reform initiatives tend to implement top-down workshops that often do not impact sustainable teacher capacity to continuously improve practice (Martin et al., 2020). Jonathan A. Supovitz (2018) describes the evidence of organizational tension that relies on such hierarchical models of administrative bureaucracy. This was true for teachers at Pinewood Lawns, as it was not that professional development opportunities were never offered—they were!—but staff's input was never asked for and momentum was short-lived. With any new initiative that was presented, teachers learned to just smile and nod, and once their doors were closed, they knew there would be no follow-up, so they would go back to what they were doing beforehand. This passionate frustration, as Kathryn Bell McKenzie and Leslie Ann Locke (2014) call it, is recognizable and refers to similar frustrations of teacher leaders who aspired to contribute but became frustrated, even within highly collaborative environments, over the lack of influence in the decision-making processes. McKenzie and

Locke (2014) further clarify teachers' frustrations in noting their wish for their roles to be more the "arm of instructional support" (p. 182). Jennie Weiner and Sarah L. Woulfin (2018) share similar teachers' frustration in schools where they lacked the necessary structures and space to transfer what they were learning in ways that would impact entire system-level changes (McKenzie & Locke, 2014). Fullan (2014) reminds instructional leaders that highly talented individuals will not remain in a noncollaborative school for very long.

More innovative approaches involve teachers becoming co-facilitators and co-learners of their own practice collaborating in teams, which leads to greater overall student achievement (Martin et al., 2020). One of the highest requests regarding teacher collaboration, however, according to William R. Johnston and Tiffany Berglund (2018) of the RAND Corporation, is time to collaborate, with structures in place that maximize resources and allow for flexibility to adapt to their needs.

Martin and colleagues (2020) argue that "building capacity by promoting teachers' individual and collective learning is an important prerequisite for a school's ability to sustain improvement" (p. 297). Indeed, *building capacity* is consistently referenced by Fullan (2014), Fullan and Quinn (2016a, 2016b), and Martin and colleagues (2020) as an essential condition for overall school improvement; according to professor of educational leadership Curt M. Adams (2013), its two most important components include effective teaching and quality learning. Instructional leaders *must* lead the learning among and for students, as well as faculty and staff; it is not only important but imperative, says educational consultant David M. Horton (2017). Fullan and Quinn (2016a) reiterate that capacity building is an approach, not a program, and delineate the skills, competencies, and knowledge that individuals and groups need to be effective.

Instructional capacity includes not only the resources within a school that enhance teaching effectiveness but the social processes that allow school professionals to facilitate professional development and build their knowledge and expertise (Adams, 2013). Researchers Frank Crowther (2011) and Joel Knudson (2013) state that high-performing schools are defined by such capacity to transfer information into knowledge and further actionable steps, allowing room for flexibility to adapt to what a school really needs. In an article for *Educational Management Administration and Leadership*, Lijuan Li, Philip Hallinger, and Allan Walker (2016) explain that successful school leadership focuses on curriculum, instruction, and learning processes, as well as staff motivation that includes capacity development, both technical and relational. Moreover, information does not simply become shared understanding or actionable implementation unless individuals and groups are willing to be vulnerable with one another (Adams, 2013). Teaching and learning are shaped by relationships built on trust, and trust comes through opportunities to exchange ideas that improve teaching and learning.

High trust, in turn, equates to an open, collaborative instructional core or relational networks. Trust increases when schools invest in the human and social enterprise, not solely an increase in new programs (Adams, 2013). Trust is an indicator of social conditions; it shows that the environment offers opportunities for dialogue that facilitates the exchange of information and transfer of knowledge indicative of a high-quality teaching and learning organization. Trust is the mediating condition through which leadership impacts continuous improvement (Adams, 2013; Li et al., 2016). Trust itself, however, does not measure the level of knowledge created by the efforts of capacity building (Adams, 2013).

Fullan (2019) and Fullan and Quinn (2016a) suggest that building internal capacity for significant change is achieved when there is coherence versus conformity—meaning that there is a shared understanding about the purpose of the work that can come only from ongoing interaction and collaboration among people *and* that these opportunities allow room for modification to adapt to the unique needs of each individual school. Conformity, on the other hand, has had a history leaning toward a more compliance-oriented, mandate-filled environment where results often are not achieved because collaboration is mostly nonexistent (Fullan & Quinn, 2016a). Schools will need to meet the needs of their students in new, more flexible, collaborative ways. Schools need instructional leaders who can build more leaders for the future, attend to more complex problems, and show a willingness to try a range of plausible solutions.

A collaborative school culture fosters teacher professional growth, and the cooperative exercise of leadership determines the approaches to professional learning that could have the most impact on the collective development of instructional practice (Martin et al., 2020). Instructional leaders need support with how to facilitate knowledge creation with trust in mind. So, let's get started!

How Do I Use a Strengths-Based Approach Toward Building Instructional Leadership Capacity?

Norms, values, trust, and commitment are instrumental to human capital geared toward developing teacher knowledge, skills, expertise, and disposition to learning (Martin et al., 2020). Leveraging collective learning, the process through which human capital is developed, depends on the interactions that develop the skill sets of each person to interact and collaborate—all of which are built on trust (Fullan, 2014; Knudson, 2013; Wieczorek & Lear, 2018). Instructional leaders need an explicit process for creating instructional leadership capacity to lead, engage, and grow professionally, and developing this process takes time (Martin et al., 2020). See figure 4.1 for a broad view of the process of capacity building.

The process of capacity building starts with providing new opportunities to learn new skills. This can begin with small conversations to plant seeds of inquiry or wonderings about what teachers want to learn more about, and can support them moving into leadership roles if they wish. The next step involves a sense of a double agenda, per se:

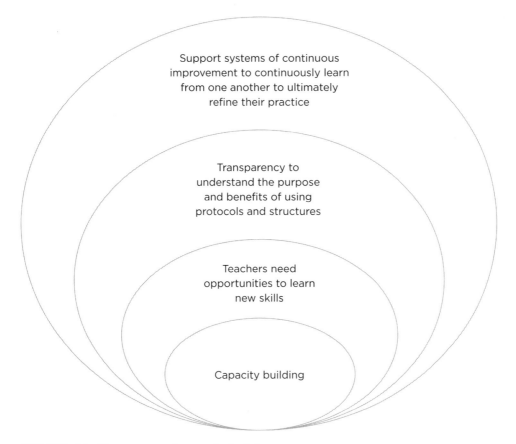

FIGURE 4.1: The process of capacity building.

understanding what you are covering in meetings, however, with an explanation of the whys behind the need for protocols and structures to facilitate new learning. It is important to be transparent regarding what these structures and protocols are and their purpose to align with each objective. Support systems of continuous improvement must be in place throughout the entire process of building capacity to continue to learn from one another during an entire school year. As I've indicated previously, instructional leaders' assumption of staff's positive intentions is critical in building trust, and this goes for building capacity as well. That is, building capacity within a school must begin with instructional leaders' believing that educators are doing the very best they know how. This approach reminds me of what Malcolm Gladwell (2019) refers to as *defaulting to truth*, rather than assuming deception, in your encounters with others. Though on some occasions individuals may let you down, you ultimately must assume faculty and staff are honest and well intentioned in their work because "there is no advantage to spending your time scrutinizing the words and behaviors of those around you" (Gladwell, 2019, p. 100). In fact, as psychologist Tim Levine explains, "What we get in exchange for being vulnerable . . . is efficient communication and social coordination. The benefits are huge and the costs are trivial in comparison" (as cited in Gladwell, 2019, p. 101). Indeed, the work of leadership coach Karen Anderson (n.d.) supports the idea that instructional leaders who take seriously this social contract as they call on others to engage in work and accomplish new goals are better positioning themselves to build trust; nurture strong, long-lasting relationships on a solid foundation; and develop the capacity of those they lead to be successful in meeting challenges.

With this approach, capacity building can start to take form with structured support, and ultimately leadership can be flattened. And with more transparency about the overall purpose of protocols, teachers can feel more open to learning from one another to improve their practices. Together, this will help institutions move away from a more traditional hierarchy with administration at the top, followed by department chairs, and teachers at the bottom. Where deeply rooted hierarchical structures and cultures exist, a teacher leader's ability to influence instructional growth is minimized (Nguyen & Hunter, 2018; Supovitz, 2018; Weiner & Woulfin, 2018). Distributed leadership systems can include models of leadership that move away from a more traditional hierarchy that can include more flat and reciprocal structures (Mulford & Silins, 2011). A flattened model increases investment in each individual's ability and permission in being a decision maker, where each individual has the freedom to communicate across rather than up or down. Investments in adult learning leads to powerful changes in student learning and achievement. A shared sense of purpose and a more collaborative culture are also elements evident within more distributed models of leadership (Marks & Printy, 2003).

Goal: Assess Before You Assemble Your Instructional Leadership Teams

So, your mindset is grounded in positive intentions and a more collaborative approach. Now what? First, go slow to go fast. Remember to take inventory of what practices are already in place. It is very common, given frequent administrative turnover, that both good and bad initiatives disappear. However, teacher turnover, reassignments, and transfers often occur too, so certain school activities or strategies may also leave with teachers who originally brought them to the school. Take note not only of what such practices and initiatives were but of who was involved, why they worked well, and how their success was measured.

Try This: Create an Inventory Checklist

Before you begin in your new role as an instructional leader and throughout your first few weeks in this position, it will be imperative to use figure 4.2 to take inventory of your school's practices to build capacity. (See page 85 for a reproducible version of this figure.) If you have already started at your school, take inventory once more. Place a check or a question mark next to each question to consider or make a note to remind yourself to find out this information soon. Note, too, that this process of taking inventory can simply be recording informal observations as you learn more about your school or district.

Questions to Consider	✓ or ?	Notes
How old or young is the school?	?	I have no idea. Check the website or School Accountability Report Card?
How long has the superintendent been in their role?	✓	One year; previous Assistant Supt.
What are this year's and last year's district goals?	✓/?	I know two—technology and writing. I know there's a third. Ask Resource Teacher.
Who are the members of the school board?	✓/?	I know one of them. Look up board meeting notes.
Is there a local partnering university or college?	✓	yes! I know this university. I wonder which departments partner with us.
Who are community partners, organizations, or businesses?	?	we have a local library, that's all I know about
Who was the previous principal? How many years were they the principal?	✓	One principal prior—one year; one other principal prior—twelve years
Are there assistant principals? If so, how many? How long have they been in their positions, and what are their main duties?	✓/?	None prior—new position created last year—duties not sure
Has there ever been an instructional coach?	✓	No instructional coaches in this district; resource teachers exist in elementary levels and TOSAs in secondary; roles are not clear
Who does the leadership team consist of?	✓/?	There's a list with an agenda from previous years, but no clear roles – who teaches what?
How many teachers are on staff?	✓	seventeen
Do you have a counselor, social worker, or psychologist?	✓/?	Part-time counselor; no social worker and one psychologist. Can we get a social worker on campus as a position here? How is that decided?

FIGURE 4.2: Inventory checklist for instructional leaders.

continued →

How many education specialists are there, and what is the caseload ratio?	✓/?	Five; are they divided up by grade? What is the caseload ratio? Different from elementary to secondary? Is there a District Director that oversees Special Education?
How many classified staff are there?	✓	Fourteen
How many grade levels does the school have?	✓	Ten (PreK–grade 8)
How many departments does the school have?	✓	Four
What are this year's identified areas for needed improvement (school goals)? Last year's?	✓	Writing—the actual writing process, vocabulary, and PBIS
Do you have a copy of the master schedule? How long has it been in place?	✓	Twenty years
What digital platforms are used for instruction? For grades? For assessments?	✓	iREADY; EM4; Aeries
Is this a 1:1 district or school?	✓	No; they do have Chromebooks in each classroom, however
Is there a strategic plan in place for technology? What about for distance or hybrid learning?	✓	No strategic plan for technology exists; DL plans exist—different schedules for each level (elementary/middle/high) and hybrid
What publishers and curricula are used?	✓	Heinemann, Wonders
What other departments provide professional development? How is it delivered? Evaluations? Feedback?	✓	TOSAs; no one on campus has ever provided PD
What leadership training has already taken place? When? What were the outcomes?	✓	None
Has a survey been given to teachers about what they want to focus on?	✓	Not yet. I do know one has been created.

Additional notes:

More specific wonderings I have:

Is there a different schedule for Thursdays? Minimum Days—every week?

Where would I find team notes from previous years? Paper or online?

Figure 4.3 is an example of the process for continuous improvement that serves as a guide for instructional leaders to build instructional leadership. Instructional leaders are often hired to be a part of the school because of the unique lens they bring. However, the purpose of the inventory checklist is to prevent the introduction of a practice that is already in place and to provide an opportunity for instructional leaders to hear about why strategies might not have been successful in the past. In other words, listen and learn first! This overall coherent approach to building capacity is grounded in personal and professional development of each educator, with a focus on increasing collective and individual efficacy, team collaboration, continuous improvement, and empowerment to ultimately increase student achievement, trust, and instructional leadership skills. This framework offers a flexible guide to adapt to the needs of your school and strategically keep moving forward.

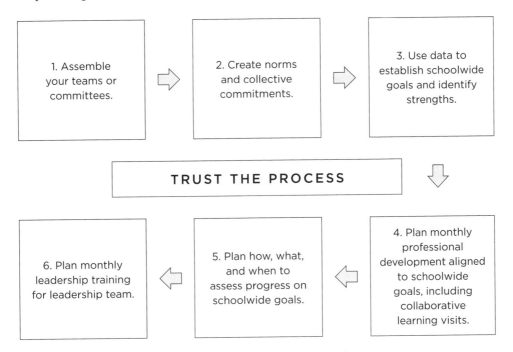

FIGURE 4.3: Process for continuous improvement.

The tools within each step are intended to guide the work with your respective teams of teachers, as well as provide structure to increase equitable participation, ensure active listening skills are used, build relationships, and increase overall equitable outcomes for teachers so that adults in the school foster an environment centered on trust.

Try This: Assemble Your Teams or Committees

Committees or teams must be established. If committees and teams are already in place, revisit the purpose of each committee or team and its respective members for equitable representation of your entire school. Of course, it's easier to keep standing committees each year, but consider reviewing why some committees exist and whether they are aligned to both district and school goals. Figure 4.4 is an example of a committee sign-up sheet review that is updated and merged, comparing two years at a glance. (See page 88 for a reproducible version of this figure.)

Our District Goals: Reading and Academic Vocabulary Our School Goals: Reading and Academic Vocabulary and PBIS	Our District Goals: Writing and EL Strategies Our School Goals: The Writing Process, AVID Strategies, & Restorative Practices
Example of Committee Sign-Up Sheet	**Example of Updated Committee Sign-Up Sheet**
AVID Leadership Team (Identification of specific number of teachers from certain grade ranges—for example, 1 teacher K-3, 1 teacher 4-6, 1 teacher 7-8) Representatives will attend monthly after-school meetings, share AVID strategies at staff meetings, and assist AVID site coordinators with the certification process.	**AVID Leadership Team** Merged with Leadership Team
Leadership Team Representatives will attend monthly meetings to discuss progress, goals, or concerns that apply to grade level or school. Monthly meetings on Tuesdays or Wednesdays.	**Leadership Team** Representatives will attend monthly meetings to discuss progress, goals, or concerns that apply to grade level or school. AVID strategies and certification will be reviewed during monthly meetings that will take place on Tuesdays.
Reading Committee Representatives review data to monitor words read and organize end-of-year events. Representatives meet monthly on Wednesdays.	**Reading Committee** Merged with Literacy Committee
Safety Committee Meets quarterly to organize and update emergency supplies, plans, and procedures.	**Safety Committee** Merged with PBIS Committee
PBIS Committee Representatives attend monthly team meetings at the site to review data and assess the site's progress in PBIS.	**PBIS Committee** Representatives attend monthly team meetings at the site to review data and assess the site's progress in PBIS. Organizes and updates emergency supplies, plans, and procedures.

FIGURE 4.4: Committee sign-up sheet review.

Certain committees may or may not serve the needs or goals of the school, and this is a good time to consider whether they should stay in place. Ask for input. Are the same people serving on the same committees year after year? Unchecked, this practice can result in favoritism and lead to a culture of mistrust. Consider rotating members of each committee if this is the case at your school.

Goal: Instructional Leadership Teams in Place? Now, Cocreate the How and the What of Strengths-Based Capacity Building

Congratulations! You have a leadership team in place. Before you jump in, remember that guiding the team will not be simply about what you present throughout the team meetings. Consider three things: (1) it's not just what you present, but how you facilitate each meeting is also important; (2) keep in mind that how this team works will be a model for someone on that team to follow your lead when they put their own leadership team in place, and it will be important to encourage their confidence or what DeWitt (2022) refers to as the work of leaders to develop leadership self-efficacy; and (3) you're ready to start, which means you start with *how* you are going to work together on this team with a laser focus on building a collaborative culture focused on strengths. Kouzes and Posner (2017) remind leaders that in order to create a culture of collaboration, there needs to be an understanding of what the group needs to do and a focus on building their team around a common purpose, making trust and teamwork high priorities.

Try This: Create and Use Norms Intentionally and Develop Collective Commitments

Collective commitments are a set of statements created by your team to reflect what you believe in and are committed to as a school. Norms are also collectively created. The purpose of norms is to help set a clear purpose for how the work will get done. Norms are intended to be referenced often to keep the group on task. According to Knight (2016) and Richard DuFour, Rebecca DuFour, Robert Eaker, Thomas W. Many, and Mike Mattos (2016), norms should be intentionally reviewed at the beginning of every meeting to reinforce how the work is going to be done throughout the meeting.

Instructional leaders, however, should not just hand a team or committee a list of norms to use (DuFour et al., 2016; Knight, 2016). For norms to be effective, team members must have a say in creating them (Graham & Ferriter, 2010; Knight, 2016). It is helpful for you to share a variety of examples of norms, however, and you can always ask staff to identify a few norms to focus on for that day's meeting. Similarly, in the process of cocreating a school's collective commitments, it is not helpful to simply cut and paste another school's statements, because each school culture's unique collective commitments should reflect what you value as a school. Norms, or your working agreements, will serve as reminders to focus on the purpose of the work and are helpful especially throughout the process of creating collective commitments. Both norms and collective commitments together set the foundation to move forward, stay focused, and also refer back while you engage in the process involved in building capacity. To begin brainstorming ideas for your school's collective commitments, consider the following questions. Jot down your thoughts individually on a sticky note. Then post your sticky notes under each question as a group to see what you individually value and what you value as a whole. You may need to sort your individual sticky notes into broader categories.

- What do you value?
- What do you believe in?
- What does our school collectively believe in?

Creating the collective commitments for Pinewood Lawns Middle School took at least two full meetings from beginning to completion, a pack of delicious-smelling markers, a little soft music, and chart paper—and although it was not easy, it was well worth the time investment. Each chart paper featured different questions, and after teachers posted their answers on sticky notes beneath the corresponding questions, the responses were sorted by topic to create statements.

Here are some of the questions staff addressed.

- How do we effectively behave as a team?
- What is the most important thing for us to tackle now, and why?
- What are the expectations for all staff?
- What does success look like at our school?

One of the questions that prompted a much deeper conversation was the question regarding expectations for staff members. Many teachers shared that their job was to teach their content and that social and emotional learning was not their responsibility, while other teachers felt the complete opposite. Staff brought up an extensive range of topics in this regard. During this conversation, I reminded teachers that no decisions would be made throughout that part of the process, so they could each state their opinions and thoughts openly. Figure 4.5 is the completed set of collective commitments that this school created.

Try This: Use Data to Establish Schoolwide Goals and Identify Strengths

Instructional leaders will find it helpful to create a targeted yet flexible plan with schoolwide goals for increasing student achievement. Believing that people can succeed is only part of the equation; clear desired outcomes need to be identified. Goals provide

We believe . . .

- In building positive relationships with students to increase work ethic and motivation to ultimately become productive and responsible citizens
- That every staff member must create a respectful environment to empower and nurture academic and personal growth in every student
- In collaborating with colleagues in an open-minded and solution-oriented manner and in holding each other accountable for mutually agreed-on decisions
- In holding all students to high academic and behavioral expectations
- In creating an engaging classroom environment through differentiated learning strategies, supported by technology, in order to meet most individual student needs to prepare students for high school and beyond
- That each of our faculty and staff should actively listen, share ideas and concerns freely, and demonstrate appreciation for and recognition of others, so that through the examples we set, we will model cooperation, trust, and respect to our students and each other
- That all parent partnerships are important elements in supporting and motivating our students, as frequent and open communication with parents increases their investment and participation in our school community

Source: Herndon Middle School; Columbus Tustin Middle School. Used with permission.

FIGURE 4.5: Final copy of collective commitments.

teachers with a set of standards that focus everyone's efforts (Kouzes & Posner, 2017). Without a goal, it is very likely that no meaningful action will occur (Knight, 2018).

Guiding teachers while explaining the plan will allow them to see how the work connects to a larger purpose and will inspire them to work together to achieve a common goal (Kouzes & Posner, 2017). For example, what sources of data are available? Using only achievement data from statewide assessments is not a good idea because state assessments do not reflect the entire picture of what students learned. What qualitative data might you have access to? From what sources? Conduct a data audit. The following list offers a few sources of data to consider.

- Attendance rates
- Test scores
- Student, staff, and parent survey results
- Graduation rates
- Climate survey results

Once you have collected various forms of data, ask for any additional input. Once there is a consensus, move your team into reviewing a sample protocol to use to have a dialogue about data with a lens on a realistic and measurable plan for what to do with what you learn from the data. See figure 4.6 (page 76) for four steps to help you and staff unpack data. (See page 89 for a reproducible version of this figure.)

This protocol is used to build understanding of everyone's perspective about data so that you walk away with an actionable plan to do something with it that is measurable. The purpose for data is to analyze it and use it to improve teaching and learning. We will also work together to try to avoid judgments. We encourage everyone to speak up. Please remember that we want to focus on data-based statements. Let's focus on causes of student performance and offer plausible solutions together.

Performance

1. How do you think your students performed overall, and why?

I think students did really well on the three branches of government, but not so great on the concept of checks and balances. I don't think they understand who checks what just yet.

2. What specific questions do you think they did well on? Why?

I think they know who leads each branch really well. The last video clip we watched, they really liked, and they talked about it afterwards. I think they might still be wondering what the process is for when a bill becomes a law, however.

3. What specific questions do you think they struggled with? Why?

Maybe question #5, where they are asking about executive power. They confused that with the Supreme Court. Maybe it's the vocabulary words used? Not sure.

Analyze

1. Let's take a look at our data. See how students did and jot down a few statements about what you see using numbers only.

Only 2 of my students distinguished revising and editing with the right example. I wonder if they know how to explain it better? 75% of students identified the writing process in the correct order.

Celebrate

1. What can you celebrate? Why do you think students did well in this area or on this question?

They understand the executive branch really well. Maybe it's because of the news lately. They seem to be well-versed on the roles of the President.

2. What instructional strategies were helpful across the board?

We used sentence frames a lot to support their thinking and helped English learners a lot too. The visuals with the branches of government helped everyone remember.

Knowledge

1. What are you going to do differently with what you learned?

I think I need to find more current events to make the material relevant. There's a lot in the news right now that I can pull examples from that they would love. Especially Supreme Court cases. They get really excited and sometimes angry about certain issues. Maybe we can have a debate or something?

2. When will you try that, and how will you know it worked?

I think I should do it soon. I should survey students about the topic they want to do a debate on and integrate the branches of government and their jobs in it. I wonder what roles of the government they would change and why. I'll assess them after our debate and see what they learned from it to compare their learning.

3. What additional support might you need to implement this?

I need more content support. I think I should bring this up at our next department meeting and ask what everyone else uses to teach this unit and next.

4. Who might serve as extra support in that instructional, tech, or content area?

Instructional coach! I need to email her! And, tech support. I wonder if she knows of any good videos I can use and how I can download them or post them to my platform. Maybe Edpuzzle has some videos?

5. How might you include students in creating a measurable action plan or goal?

I think I need to include them on creating goals for what they think they will get on the next assessment and ask them what strategies they might use. Maybe a fun competition between periods. They love a good competition.

FIGURE 4.6: Four steps to un-PACK data.

There are two important points to emphasize. First, it will be important to model the facilitation of a protocol to look at data and remember that you are guiding the process toward plausible solutions. You must give yourself and the team permission not to finalize a plan immediately. Be clear about that before you begin this process.

School goals do not have to be based solely on deficits; they can be based on strengths that you want to continue to improve. Building capacity requires consistently spending time celebrating strengths, as you will want to further explore *why* certain areas are stronger than others. Give yourself permission to keep goals consistent from year to year if you still need improvement in that area. However, keep it to no more than three goals. See figure 4.7 for a chart to aid you in keeping track of and aligning your school goals from year to year with a strategy for each goal, as well as the best tech tools to implement to leverage each goal. (See page 91 for a reproducible version of this figure.)

Second, this is another place where you begin the process of identifying teachers' strengths and empowering them to realize the capacity within themselves and others that might have previously gone unnoticed. In identifying which strategies are being used, talk to your team to rate their proficiency with each goal (as introduced in figure 3.2, page 58) and ask whether they are willing to share their expertise for future professional development opportunities.

Try This: Plan Monthly Professional Development Aligned to Schoolwide Goals, Including Collaborative Learning Visits

A rough draft of a timeline of topics for each month's professional development should be aligned and organized according to your school goals. Alongside the larger topics planned for monthly professional development, five to ten dates throughout the school year can also be selected, depending on the number of teachers you have and your budget, to offer a more tailored form of professional development: collaborative learning visits, wherein teachers visit one another's classrooms to observe best teaching and learning practices.

During CLVs, both the visiting teacher and the hosting teacher learn, and it is not considered a formal or evaluative observation—hence the word *visit*. It is important to note the difference between CLVs and lesson studies. Although lesson study is an excellent practice with significant evidence regarding its benefits, CLVs are not the Japanese method of teacher-led research where, according to educators Catherine C. Lewis and Jacqueline Hurd (2011), teachers research the problem of practice, plan one lesson or series of lessons together, and then observe one teacher deliver the lesson followed by a reflection. The benefit of CLVs begins with the purpose. Since teachers rarely get out of their classrooms, they do not get to see best practices in action. Providing an opportunity for peer-to-peer observation has a profound impact not only on student achievement but also on teacher collaboration (Marzano, 2011).

I introduced CLVs to Pinewood Lawns Middle School and outlined the following general objectives that you, too, can relay to your team so the benefits of the exercise are crystal clear. The objectives are:

- To provide an alternative form of tailored professional development
- To see best practices and student learning
- To collect evidence of engagement in learning
- To ultimately implement new ideas with best practices in your own classroom

School Year	School Goal	Strategies or Methods to Address Each Goal	Technology to Leverage	Dates to Check in and With What Data
2020–2021	1. Increase English learners' academic language development, achievement, reclassification rates with a focus on a signature strategy targeting Academic Vocabulary & Collaborative Conversations.	Frayer Model • Increase student collaborative conversations using sentence frames and four corners within Jamboard. • Continually analyze data to identify areas of need and growth. • Administrators do presentations on the importance of yearly language exams and celebrate redesignated ELs schoolwide. Also share with parents at Parent Coffees. • Use schoolwide CLVs to share strategies that are working well.	Pear Deck, create GIFs to animate visuals, use www .wordhippo.com to help with antonyms and synonyms	Quarterly at our faculty meeting: • Bring student samples of Frayers or teaches can digitally share them with our resource teacher to print. How are they changing over time? • Let's use a different protocol each time using student samples across our TK–8. We can use a gallery walk (vertical articulation). • Add CLV pictures to Eagle Eye Weekly Bulletin.
	2. Increase the use of inquiry-based questioning to move away from "rescuing" students and allow for productive struggle.	Encourage collaborative conversations using leveled questions from AVID.	Google Docs to share the types of questions we will ask to invite productive struggle. Classified staff has requested a ring to carry with them to help them remember what questions to ask as well.	Quarterly. What questions are we using? What success have we found with them? What's not working? What shift have we noticed in students? How will we hold ourselves accountable to using our new questioning techniques? Share out what's working.
	3. Increase the use of PBIS strategies, specifically restorative justice practices, to help students solve issues between peers.	Administrators and counselor can model how to use this strategy in class with elementary school levels. How can students conduct a classroom restorative justice circle to bring calm and peace to their classroom and create a classroom of respectful behavior for all?	Video to show students what this looks like first. Encourage students to "catch" students being kind. Admin can take pictures (with permission) and include in weekly shoutout (digitally).	Monthly data pulls. How many discipline referrals are there? What grades? What areas of the school? Might we have a model restorative justice classroom?

FIGURE 4.7: Align your school goal and strategy for each goal and tech tool to leverage.

Additionally, there are three main components of CLVs: (1) the planning phase; (2) the actual classroom visit; and (3) the debrief, which can be facilitated alongside an instructional coach (if your site is fortunate enough to have one). Figure 4.8 delineates specific questions teachers should ask themselves during each phase. (Note that questions should be focused on the school goals and the following bulleted list should be shared, as they introduce CLVs to the school.)

Before: Planning Phase	• What is one strategy or method you want to implement in your classroom? • What is your greatest fear about trying this strategy or method?
During: Classroom Visit	• What are the students doing? • What are the content and language objectives of the lesson? How do you know?
After: Debrief	• What structures, protocols, or scaffolds appear to be in place for collaborative conversations among students? • What is one instructional strategy, method, or activity that you will bring back to your classroom? • What support might you need from administration or a coach to do so?

FIGURE 4.8: Questions to ask during each phase of CLVs.

Be sure to model correct terminology for teachers to use before, during, and after CLVs—though during is most crucial, as nonevaluative language is required (see table 4.1). There will be things classroom visitors *like* around the classroom, but crafting statements around likes is more subjective and judgmental. The emphasis of the visit is on the instructional practices with a focus on what students are doing.

TABLE 4.1: CLVs—Say This, Not That

Say This	**Not That**
Objective	Subjective or Evaluative
I notice . . . Students are . . . I observed . . .	I really like . . . I think . . . Have you considered . . .

For the debrief, questions can involve what might work in their own classroom and how they might implement it. Also, depending on how you coordinate CLVs, there may be a small expense required in setting up substitutes, or one substitute who can transition from one class to another on a given day.

CLVs are the turning point in the process of building instructional leadership capacity. You will see a shift in leadership as CLVs not only help flatten the school's leadership model but build confidence in teachers as they begin to fully appreciate their own strengths. The multiplier effect will be palpable as a number of teachers observe new instructional practices and try them across campus. As teachers ask more questions about certain practices, conversations will tend to happen horizontally, versus from the top down.

We cannot leave the topic of CLVs without a conversation about relationship building. CLVs create the conditions for teachers to realize their own capacity and can help create a culture of mutual trust in your school. CLVs not only serve as a tailored form of professional development; they are also an investment of time for teachers to deepen professional relationships, which in turn builds trust. Inviting someone into your classroom requires trust, and when you do not know people very well and still invite them to enter your room, how you engage when you are in there can build stronger relationships.

Try This: Identify How and When to Assess Progress on Schoolwide Goals

School goals are important to plan and set in motion, but there is as much of an implementation gap as there is an achievement gap. There is no shortage of what does work in education—only a failure to implement and then monitor progress. Calendaring check-in dates along with assessments is helpful. Check-ins should stand as scheduled monthly meetings within your leadership committee, and informal observations should include feedback on each of the school goal areas as well. Monthly professional development can leverage this feedback, and most important, celebrate successes and highlights from CLVs during these moments.

At Pinewood Lawns Middle School, we collected student writing samples across grade levels. This provided an opportunity for vertical articulation to assess how what they were integrating for teaching writing was going and gauge what their next steps would be to fine-tune instruction to improve learning, specifically with a focus on three categories divided among grade levels: (1) terminology, (2) tools and resources used, and (3) strategies. The focus of inquiry started with a question of "What are the components of efficient writing instruction at your respective grade level?"

Try This: Set Up Monthly Leadership Training for Leadership Team

This final exercise is the most important for any instructional leader in *any* school setting. It is essential to provide specific leadership training to a leadership team if you want to not only build instructional leadership capacity but also empower leaders to create a strong culture of mutual trust. There are a variety of skills to learn, from listening more effectively (which is a game changer in the process of building trust) to fostering facilitation skills to build consensus, increasing instructional and technological skills, and understanding overall how to effectively coach and build capacity in others. Invite one of your members of your leadership team to facilitate a meeting so they can put some of these leadership skills in practice with your physical presence to support them.

To build leadership skills in your staff, begin by modeling them through daily interactions with faculty and staff. There must be a common understanding that great leaders want to make a difference versus just making a name for themselves. Teachers know whether you are simply in your position to get to the next one. However, true instructional leaders are there to serve others and want to invest in others to build on their strengths. Taking the time to share leadership research with practical skills will make a significant difference in your schools. One way you can do this is to bring in choices of articles on leadership skills to read with your team or provide a choice of two for your staff to read. Use a facilitation strategy to engage in conversation about the article, and emphasize what you are doing throughout the meeting so they understand how you are trying to facilitate it. Share research while modeling how to lead such a discussion.

VIRTUAL LEARNING LIGHTBULB

Online meetings can sometimes get a bit monotonous, especially if you are at home for an extended period of time and need a break from more traditional meetings. Provide options to develop leadership skills by utilizing breakout rooms in your meetings with different topics in each room. Perhaps you can share a different article to read or a short video clip to watch that reinforces either the same or various other leadership skills. Have the entire team come back and share out what conversations were had to ensure there is diversity with the methods you build capacity with during virtual learning times.

School Scenario

I was a coach of coaches at a new school. The first few meetings I observed at this school were administrative. I remember listening to an almost twenty-minute conversation about why the student council members, rather than the custodians, should pick up trash after the dance, followed by another twenty-minute conversation about what the principal could do to quiet down the way-too-loud lunches. Information was usually given out of order, without much dialogue regarding data or instructional practices. Then came the shift toward these new meetings where we started by reviewing norms and clearly written objectives so that everyone knew what the topics would be and what they needed to accomplish by the end of the meeting. The meetings were no longer a space to discuss traditional department chair tasks, randomly vent about problems, or veer off into tangential conversations. The focus was now on adult professional learning. The result, after a full year, was a shift from administrative tasks to discussions about the staff's strongest instructional strategies, supporting data, and what was working across the board. It became clear that efficacy increased over time within each teacher—and trust was building. The traditional leadership hierarchy naturally flattened. Staff had conversations across the board rather than simply up or down. Various levels of expert groups began to form. This process reemphasized to me the importance of adult learning theory—that for adult learners to truly be engaged and consider personal and professional development worthy of their time, their strengths and needs must be accounted for in the planning stages so that the professional development is both meaningful and applicable to their current roles.

Conclusion

Building instructional capacity and creating systems and protocols take time, and mean that when performance is expected from you, you also have an equal responsibility to provide the capacity to meet that expectation. This is an environment that will create a culture of reflection, collaboration, and continuous improvement (Fullan & Quinn, 2016b; Knudson, 2013). The real measure of an instructional leader is beyond student achievement scores; it is how many leaders have been further developed after the leader is gone (Fullan, 2019). The process of building capacity does not happen overnight, but the result is worth every moment you've spent planning and thoughtfully implementing structures and skills to cultivate a culture of collaboration, improved relationships, solid trust, and enhanced leadership skills.

Hearing and seeing confidence increase among teachers is the greatest reward. Throughout this process at Pinewood Lawns Middle School, trust was garnered mutually, and it was palpable. While this process provides structure, trust was built by the conversations that happened throughout the process. Protocols became internalized over time. Teachers and teacher leaders became more confident in their abilities and felt more confident in speaking up about them.

Doubts may run through your mind in trying to stay the course. It is easy to throw in the towel when things get complicated and teachers and instructional leaders get stuck in problems versus solutions. However, each step in this process works. It has worked for the most complicated of teams I have worked with. But it requires patience, and sometimes extra good humor. At Pinewood Lawns Middle School, we came up with a fun word to use when we felt stuck or derailed and needed to get back on track—*llamas*. At the end of a long, tiring meeting, someone would say, "Llamas!" We'd all laugh hysterically, and get completely off task, but ultimately it renewed our energy and got us back on track. I believe in laughter. If needed, find your *llamas* to get your team back on track. This work is hard, but the payoff is

The applicable **Educator Spotlights** in the appendix at the end of this book (page 118) further this focus.

that the process inspires new leaders and strengthens veteran leaders. It increases *trust*, and as you go slow to go fast, you will ultimately create memories that will last a lifetime and empower the next generation of leaders. The following reflection questions focus on the process of developing your strengths and those of the people with whom you work.

REFLECTION QUESTIONS

Review and record your responses to the reflection questions so you can refer back to them periodically and track your progress in building trust.

1. What structures do you already have in place toward building instructional leadership capacity, based on strengths, with trust in mind?
2. What personal strengths of yours will enable you to maximize your staff's strengths?
3. What will you need to pay attention to in yourself and others as you begin this process?
4. What's one new thing you learned from this chapter about how to build instructional leadership capacity?
5. Out of all the strategies in this chapter, which one will you implement right away, and why?

A CHECKLIST OF ACTION STEPS

Check off each of the following items as you complete it.

☐ I have reviewed the inventory checklist.

☐ I have identified at least one new structure to implement with my team.

☐ I have a plan in place to create collective commitments with my team.

☐ The strategy I will use to hold myself accountable toward building instructional leadership capacity is _____.

☐ I will gauge my progress for building both instructional leadership capacity and trust throughout the year on a _____ basis and measure that growth by _____.

Inventory Checklist for Instructional Leaders

Questions to Consider	✓ or ?	Notes
How old or young is the school?		
How long has the superintendent been in their role?		
What are this year's and last year's district goals?		
Who are the members of the school board?		
Is there a local partnering university or college?		
Who are community partners, organizations, or businesses?		
Who was the previous principal? How many years were they the principal?		
Are there assistant principals? If so, how many? How long have they been in their positions, and what are their main duties?		

Has there ever been an instructional coach?		
Who does the leadership team consist of?		
How many teachers are on staff?		
Do you have a counselor, social worker, or psychologist?		
How many education specialists are there, and what is the caseload ratio?		
How many classified staff are there?		
How many grade levels does the school have?		
How many departments does the school have?		
What are this year's identified areas for needed improvement (school goals)? Last year's?		

Trust as the Core of Instructional Leadership • © 2022 Solution Tree Press • SolutionTree.com
Visit **go.SolutionTree.com/leadership** to download this free reproducible.

Do you have a copy of the master schedule? How long has it been in place?		
What digital platforms are used for instruction? For grades? For assessments?		
Is this a 1:1 district or school?		
Is there a strategic plan in place for technology? What about for distance or hybrid learning?		
What publishers and curricula are used?		
What other departments provide professional development? How is it delivered? Evaluations? Feedback?		
What leadership training has already taken place? When? What were the outcomes?		
Has a survey been given to teachers about what they want to focus on?		
Additional notes:		

Committee Sign-Up Sheet Review

Our District Goals Last Year:	Our District Goals This Year:
Our School Goals Last Year:	Our School Goals This Year:
Example of Committee Sign-Up Sheet	**Example of Updated Committee Sign-Up Sheet**
Name of Committee or Team: _____	Name of Committee or Team: _____
Name of Committee or Team: _____	Name of Committee or Team: _____
Name of Committee or Team: _____	Name of Committee or Team: _____
Name of Committee or Team: _____	Name of Committee or Team: _____
Name of Committee or Team: _____	Name of Committee or Team: _____

Four Steps to Un-PACK Data

This protocol is used to build understanding of everyone's perspective about data so that you walk away with an actionable plan to do something with it that is measurable. The purpose for data is to analyze it and use it to improve teaching and learning. We will also work together to try to avoid judgments. We encourage everyone to speak up. Please remember that we want to focus on data-based statements. Let's focus on causes of student performance and offer plausible solutions together.

Performance:

1. How do you think your students performed overall, and why?

_____

_____

_____

2. What specific questions do you think they did well on? Why?

_____

_____

_____

3. What specific questions do you think they struggled with? Why?

_____

_____

_____

Analyze:

1. Let's take a look at our data. See how students did and jot down a few statements about what you see using numbers only.

_____

_____

Celebrate:

1. What can you celebrate? Why do you think students did well in this area or on this question?

_____

_____

_____

2. What instructional strategies were helpful across the board?

_____

_____

_____

Knowledge:

1. What are you going to do differently with what you learned?

_____

_____

_____

2. When will you try that, and how will you know it worked?

_____

_____

_____

3. What additional support might you need to implement this?

_____

_____

_____

4. Who might serve as extra support in that instructional, tech, or content area?

_____

_____

_____

5. How might you include students in creating a measurable action plan or goal?

_____

_____

_____

Align Your School Goal and Strategy for Each Goal and Tech Tool to Leverage

School Year	School Goal	Strategies or Methods to Address Each Goal	Technology to Leverage	Dates to Check in and With What Data

CHAPTER 5

Unpack Necessary Conversations With Care

As elementary school principal Bryan McLain (2011) concisely puts it, "Some of the most costly conversations are the ones that never happen" (p. 60). Think about your school and all the different people you communicate with daily. Think about a conversation you need to have with a certain person—say, for example, someone made a concerning statement that made you tilt your head and wonder exactly what that person meant, or perhaps a conversation simply feels unfinished in a way. You need to address a topic of concern with someone, and you're either avoiding it or planning to keep it clinical. What happened between the two of you? How long have you been avoiding this conversation? How many times have you told yourself to talk to this person and then, for whatever reason, you talked yourself out of it? That feeling of unfinished business between the two of you may never disappear until you have that difficult yet necessary conversation. And more important, avoidance or further mismanagement of the conversation will cost you the trust you've worked so hard to establish—and likely more.

According to researcher Maggie Farrell (2015), all organizations, by their very nature, will incur conflict, and individuals will need to negotiate their differences. Conflict itself surfaces from common sources, such as poor choice of words, unclear roles, and unclear responsibilities, to name a few (Horton, 2017). The Ontario Principals' Council (OPC, 2011) defines associated challenging conversations as an interaction between two or more parties characterized by elevated emotional intensity, differing viewpoints, and perceived high stakes for at least one person. The concept of emotional intensity is key, as it refers to the anxiety, anticipation, or even fear one person may experience before or during a conversation that can promote school improvement (OPC, 2011). Similarly, author and educational presenter Jennifer Abrams (2016) identifies "hard conversations" as those that describe the impact of current and future behaviors. Overall, I prefer to refer to these conversations strictly as *necessary* both because they need to happen and because framing them as *difficult* or *hard* before they even begin isn't particularly helpful. While educators face several challenges, we assume that our conversations will be challenging. We already assume that we can't or won't come to consensus when a resolution is in fact possible. What if the conversations aren't difficult? What if everything goes well? What if such conversations are so transformative that we wish we hadn't avoided them for so long?

Author and CEO coach Kim Scott (2019) emphasizes the *radical candor* that undergirds necessary conversations. That is, they require leaders to both genuinely care about the teachers on the other end and be direct in order to build trust and open communication to achieve results (Scott, 2019). But instructional leaders need the *skills* to initiate such conversations. This chapter provides an examination of these skills, and guidelines to confidently tap into this radical candor, as well as options for planning and how-tos for navigation.

Why Unpack Necessary Conversations With Care?

Sometimes we ignore necessary conversations because we are unable to act; as instructional leaders, we are aware that a conversation needs to take place, but the mere idea of initiating it can be paralyzing. Secondary school principals Dyan Harrison, Bill Ziegler, and Albert Sackey (2021) note that, other times, we ignore these conversations because of fear that we can't relate or that we'll say the wrong thing. However, Scott (2019) explains the results are often the opposite of what we fear. Conversations in general raise all types of emotions—ideas bring passion, and underneath passion are values—and several social and intellectual connections in which we can misconstrue words and meaning. Leaders cannot ignore these emotions, no matter what role they are in, as conflict is necessary to talk through (Harrison et al., 2021; Horton, 2017). Problems will not simply go away on their own; our ignoring them won't make them completely disappear (Farrell, 2015). Handling necessary conversations effectively is what builds trust, and doing so often communicates that mistreating people will not be tolerated (Horton, 2017). According to educator Michael W. Torres (2010), each conversation can nurture mutual respect, build on understanding of cultures, and create a new way to view or understand a problem or concept.

When handled poorly or not at all, conflict results in a lack of trust (Tschannen-Moran, 2014). And putting off necessary conversations that address conflict results in low morale and a sense of resentment among teachers who know that others are not working at quality level and are also not being held accountable (Farrell, 2015). Negotiating necessary conversations takes strategic, intentional effort and results in ongoing, honest dialogue—one where teachers can thrive and solutions can be co-constructed rather than imposed (Farrell, 2015; Horton, 2017). Instructional leaders who are able to navigate necessary conversations gain trust overall, yet it is also important to note that, once again, instructional leaders cannot simply be told to "go have a necessary conversation"; instructional leaders need specific guidance and support, with examples of what to say and what not to say before, during, and after the necessary conversation.

Instructional leaders also need to hear and see how various scenarios played out from the perspective and voice of leaders in both similar and different roles. For instructional leaders, avoidance isn't always about fear; that feeling of debilitation also stems from a lack of skills—not knowing where to begin, or how to have the conversation—and a lack of confidence to manage unexpected conflict that might arise within that conversation (Tschannen-Moran, 2014).

How Do I Unpack Necessary Conversations With Care?

Executive coach Susan Scott (2017) and her colleagues explore what it means to make conversations *fierce*, or real, because each person's perception of reality is part of the truth; conversations are *the* relationships between two individuals. Scott (2017) outlines the following seven principles for tackling fierce conversations. (See table 5.1, page 96, for further details on each principle.)

1. Master the courage to interrogate reality.
2. Come out from behind yourself, into the conversation, and make it real.
3. Be here, prepared to be nowhere else.
4. Tackle your toughest challenge today.
5. Obey your instincts.
6. Take responsibility for your emotional wake.
7. Let silence do the heavy lifting.

Underlying these principles are gentle reminders that are embedded within the suggested exercises in this chapter. Each of these seven principles can be shared as reminders with faculty and staff. Teachers often share that they find them useful in their meetings with parents as well.

Taking to heart Scott's (2017) seven principles helps to establish an authentic exchange between two people and bring brutally honest conversations to the surface. But it's also incredibly useful to consider Abrams's (2009, 2016) extensive work on unpacking necessary conversations. In *Having Hard Conversations* and *Hard Conversations Unpacked*, which cover her experience in working with students and transitioning to working with adults, Abrams (2009, 2016) focuses on better understanding why we don't speak up, generational filters and how they influence perceptions, and why it is our responsibility to prepare for these conversations in order to improve a culture of relational trust to tackle and improve student learning. Abrams (2016) contends that it is through relational trust that we are able to better focus on the behavior and handle task-oriented conflict and personal conflict. She also suggests taking the time to prepare for the necessary conversation by naming the problem, articulating solutions concretely, and keeping the focus on repeatable behaviors so that the other person knows the precise skills they need to be successful (Abrams, 2009). Wait time throughout the conversations is highly

TABLE 5.1: Summary of Seven Principles for Tackling Fierce Conversations

Seven Principles	What Does It Mean?	So What Should You Do?
Master the Courage to Interrogate Reality	We live in our own comfortable echo chambers, communicating most often with people who are similar to us, so we need to probe concepts outside our comfort zones—outside our own realities.	Name the issue. Check for agreement. Make a proposal.
Come Out From Behind Yourself, Into the Conversation, and Make It Real	Show up! Be your authentic self and share your real or inner thoughts and feelings.	Give yourself permission to clarify your position, state your point of view, and ask for what you want. Be specific!
Be Here, Prepared to Be Nowhere Else	Be present and curious about what the other person is going through.	Listen and be prepared to mutually share your feelings around the issues.
Tackle Your Toughest Challenge Today	Instead of prolonging the problem, confront someone's behavior.	Clarify why this issue is important for both parties.
Obey Your Instincts	Scott (2017) suggests to "have a conversation about your conversation" (p. 210). In essence, acknowledge that internal, private conversation you are carrying on and share your thoughts; sometimes being diplomatic or keeping it private keeps us from truly learning.	Value your instincts as a resource. Pay attention to and value the messages we receive from ourselves instead of fearing that you could be wrong or will offend someone.
Take Responsibility for Your Emotional Wake	"Each time we speak, send an e-mail or text, we leave an emotional wake" (Scott, 2017, p. 235). Deliver your genuine message; give to others what you want to receive and clarify your direct intent in that message.	Ask yourself, "What is the intention behind this conversation or statement?"
Let Silence Do the Heavy Lifting	Allow time to process information.	Invite the other person to share.

encouraged, too, as it keeps the conversation brief and clear (Abrams, 2016). Here are six questions that Abrams (2009, 2016) identifies as a framework to follow.

1. What is the problem?

2. What is the tentative outcome?

3. What are specific, desired behaviors connected to this outcome?

4. What knowledge and skills would the person need to have in order to adopt these behaviors?

5. What supports and strategies might I offer and use to help this person achieve the outcome?

6. What might I need, both internally and externally, to move this conversation forward?

As Scott's (2017) and Abrams's (2009, 2016) research illustrates, necessary conversations require purpose, time to reflect on what you really want as the desired outcome, consideration for what the other person might want, a road map for how you will start it, objectives, strategies to navigate, and always beginning with the end in mind. Planning a conversation is like preparing a well-designed lesson or a professional development session. There is a significant positive aspect to necessary conversations that needs to be emphasized and encouraged because it is through them that instructional leaders can negotiate sustained school improvement (OPC, 2011).

But, of course, effective leaders don't just become effective leaders without having had *many* conversations through a variety of circumstances (Farrell, 2015). In approaching any conversation, Murphy (2020) emphasizes a key concept referred to as *conversational sensitivity* as one who is not only able to pay attention to spoken words but able to pick up hidden meanings in tone. People with conversational sensitivity tend to remember what people say and tend to enjoy and elicit more than superficial chatter so people reveal more of who they are.

Conversational sensitivity relates to cognitive complexity, meaning you are open to a range of experiences and know how to navigate through contradictory views. We get better at detecting cues in conversations the more we listen to numerous people because we are exposed to more aspects of humanity, and it is this skill that exposes us to a range of opinions, beliefs, attitudes, and emotions (Murphy, 2020). Keep this concept in mind as you practice navigating necessary conversations. Bottom line: you must have more of them to get better at them.

Let's unpack necessary conversations with care and with a variety of tools and reflective questions to focus on before, during, and after each one.

Goal: Realize That Mindset Matters When Approaching Necessary Conversations

The first step to initiating necessary conversations is not jumping into them, which requires self-awareness. Know your triggers, and have a plan for when your own buttons are pushed. How will you respond rather than react? Prepare not to personalize any comments that come across as rude. How will you monitor your emotional responses? One of Freud's first students, Theodor Reik, suggested to note any feelings that bubble up from your unconscious; you must know what triggers you *well before* you attempt a necessary conversation (Murphy, 2020).

Try This: Swap Assumptions for Positive Presuppositions

Always honor the human in front of you, and always assume that each educator is doing the very best they know how. How you approach each conversation will influence the outcome; as ever, assume positive intentions. Each conversation is an opportunity to grow together and truly understand the different lenses we each see through (see table 5.2). You might learn something new or something new about that person. Be open to both.

TABLE 5.2: Assumptions Versus Positive Presuppositions

Staff Comment	Leader's Assumption	Leader's Positive Presupposition
"I absolutely disagree with holding an extra meeting after school today."	"You are not interested in supporting the school or students."	"You might have other events going on at home. I respect and value your time. Let's identify a date and time this week that might work."
"This unit is way too much, and I won't be taking the common assessment on time."	"You are being defiant and not even trying to work as a team."	"Perhaps there have not been any opportunities to backward plan together to identify essential standards to teach for this upcoming assessment."
"Why do we have to learn yet another new tech tool?"	"You want to do what you have been doing without being bothered."	"Maybe you are utilizing a tool that is already in place that has a variety of uses we don't know about yet. Teach us!"

Try This: The Human Connection Is What Matters Most

When people feel unheard and hurt, you must address them in a calm manner. Remember that you build trustworthy relationships through each conversation, one at a time. Each one, no matter how short or long, counts. Your relationships and your responsibilities as an instructional leader reinforce one another, and your ability to build trust—that human connection—determines everything (Scott, 2019). You must care enough about people that, when something is a little off and you instinctively know that something needs to be addressed, instead of avoiding the step to ask for clarification or talking yourself out of saying anything in that moment, you remind yourself that you care enough about them to approach the conversation (Knight, 2016; McLain, 2011; Scott, 2019). How will you ever move forward if you don't take the first step in trying to understand each other? Embrace the complexity of human connection and relationships.

Here are a few ways to show people you care during a necessary conversation.

o Tell them you care about your working relationship and want to find a way, together, to improve it.

o Allow them to answer fully. Listen!

o Paraphrase *first* to make sure you understand how *they* feel.

Try This: Use Coaching Mantras

It may not surprise you to know that my top three coaching mantras I keep in mind when I approach any conversation are "listen closely to the complaint for a request," "go slow to go fast," and "assume positive intentions" (Racines, 2019). No matter what topic I am approaching, these three never fail me. Here are a few other coaching mantras you might consider (in addition to any you already use).

- ○ "I keep student learning at the core of everything we do."
- ○ "I honor the person who is speaking by listening for how they feel."
- ○ "Have fun, value humor, and insist on laughing."

What mantras could align with you?

Try This: Bring Some Good, Positive Energy

When negative remarks become a preoccupation, our brains lose mental efficiency (Kouzes & Posner, 2017). Being positive opens people up, allowing them to see more options and be more resilient during times of stress, ensuring all educational partners or teachers and instructional leaders work on solutions together in a safe, collaborative manner (Kouzes & Posner, 2017). I always say to myself, each morning (it is actually a highlighted hot pink reminder on my Google Calendar on my phone that goes off as an appointment each morning at 8 a.m.), to "be the person you want to be around." I love being around positivity, so why seek it? Create it. Bring that calm, positive energy to your daily environment. It is palpable. You know that energy shift when you walk into a certain room. Remember how you do *not* want people to feel around you, so be cognizant of that. Share your outlook about necessary conversations as actions toward improvement and understanding, rather than punitive measures, to not only talk the walk but walk the talk of your school being a true learning school (Fullan, 2014). Tell your staff that you invite conversations, and actually mean it. Share what your thinking is about and how necessary they are to move forward to create the ideal school we all want to come to work to each day.

Goal: Be Prepared Before the Conversation

The anticipation of a necessary conversation might bring on stress, but taking the time to prepare for the conversation beforehand will really make all the difference during the one-to-one. Use the following exercises to help you set the tone for the conversation, provide clarity, and consider the issue from all angles, empowering you to change the trajectory of what might from the outset seem like a difficult discussion.

Try This: Review and Refer to the Norms

Norms are as critical for necessary conversations as much as they are for any meetings. Use the norms that have been cocreated by your school, and also ask to be able to add, edit, or shift any norm or focus on a specific norm for this particular meeting. Establish expectations for the agenda for your conversation regarding why you want to discuss the certain topic and refer back to your norms before you begin. Keep your norms visible during the conversation and refer to them as needed. Examples of norms that may be suggested to be added include a commitment to speak truthfully and respectfully and wait for each person to finish speaking to more consciously not interrupt each other (Tschannen-Moran, 2014).

Try This: Be Clear About Purpose and Desired Outcomes

So that you're able to remain focused on the purpose and communicate up front the desired outcomes, outline a few talking points in case you later get offtrack (Farrell, 2015; figure 5.1). (See page 107 for a reproducible version of this figure.) I recommend practicing various approaches to this conversation with a coach and if you do not have a coach, a trusted colleague, preferably one who is not at your site. I would not recommend a mutual colleague to allow for objectivity and maintain confidentiality. Ask for surprise reactions so you have an opportunity to respond in real time (Farrell, 2015).

Preparation notes for conversation with ___Anne___			
Why am I having this conversation?	**What is the desired outcome?**	**How might they react?**	**How will I respond (not *react*)?**
I feel like there's unfinished business between us. You said something at our last meeting, and I just can't get over it. You made a statement about a student and his inability to learn. It's bugging me.	I want to ask for clarification. What did she mean by her comment? I want to understand what was said and meant by it.	She could reinforce the very negative comment or not.	Assume positive intentions. Did I hear the whole intention? Go in calmly and be mindful of my facial expressions. Remember to gain clarity before anything else.

FIGURE 5.1: Notes for necessary conversations.

Try This: Consider Where the Conflict Developed and the Implications for the School

Identify the possible sources of the conflict, and plan to share them. This builds trust because you'll convey that you are genuinely trying to understand the issue from all angles. Examine the situation from different perspectives to home in on the core issue (Farrell,

2015). It is beneficial to discuss implications for the school as well. Help each other see the larger picture and who the situation affects. It is important to talk about the implications if the problem continues and the outcomes if the problem is cleared up so that in the future both implications and outcomes are considered. See figure 5.2 (page 102) for a planning template. (See page 108 for a reproducible version of this figure.)

Goal: Be Prepared During the Conversation

It's time for the conversation to begin! The following exercises will assist you in effectively conveying your identified purpose, maintaining awareness of your nonverbal communication, and choosing your words carefully to ensure the conversation remains both fruitful and respectful.

Try This: State the Purpose and Invite Clarification

Restate the purpose and desired outcome and allow time for clarification. Before the conversation continues, make sure you are both in agreement—for example, "So we both agree that the purpose of this conversation is to clarify X, and we both want to see Y as the desired outcome of this conversation today?"

Try This: Be Mindful of Your Nonverbal Communication

When people try to communicate with others, it is not only the message that matters (Maxwell, 2010). Necessary conversations are those in which feelings and attitudes may be communicated, and it is in these situations that what we say only accounts for 7 percent of what is believed, the way we say it accounts for 38 percent, and what others see accounts for 55 percent (Maxwell, 2010). Be cognizant of what your body language and unintended facial expressions are expressing while you are listening, and also be aware of what you are *not* focusing on either (your phone or the clock).

Try This: Ask More Open-Ended Questions

One of the best suggestions I have learned is to ask more open-ended questions to make sure that everything has been said. I am sure you have experienced a conversation that you had where you walked away wishing you had said just one more thing, right? Make sure you provide an opportunity to elicit as much information as possible and that time is provided to think through anything else that needs to be said. Use the prompt, "Tell me more about . . ." and be sure to ask, "What ideas do you have about solutions?"

Try This: Avoid Saying, "Don't Take This Personally"

I am guilty of saying this in the past, and now, as I look back, I understand how it is actually insulting to say this to another person. Do not tell another person how to feel or how to interpret what you say. Instead, acknowledge that you care not only about

Notes for conversation with ___Justina___ about ___use of class time___

What's the conflict?	What could be the source of the conflict? When did it develop? Write down your perspective.	What are the implications for the school? For the team?	Consider the other person's perspective. What might they say about when the conflict developed and its source?	What are possible solutions?
A teacher is upset with another teacher because she is inviting students to her classroom during instruction and the students are missing important class time.	This has been ongoing. Both teachers had a disagreement months ago about how their roles should be divided up, and instead of agreeing, they each said they are going to do it their own way without any further conversation.	The parents of students are aware that some students are being taken out, and one student told their other teacher that they are watching movies and listening to music. This has implications with parent-teacher relationships, co-teaching models in the school, and overall trust issues between teachers.	The other teacher said that this was not the entire story. This developed one day when one teacher asked them to take on additional roles when students were not understanding the material and to take them out into the hall. This created a good-cop-bad-cop scenario, and it became divisive and unequal.	Discuss the role of co-teaching and the roles that are expected from each. Review what is ideal. Review what is not working and why. How can the roles become more equitable and not feel so divisive moving forward?

FIGURE 5.2: Notes on where the conflict developed and implications for the school.

the topic of concern but about them as a person (Scott, 2019). For example, instead of saying, "Don't take this personally, but _____," say, "I understand that you are angry about _____. Help me understand why." In fact, in this situation, try to cut down on your use of the word *but*—for example, "I really wanted to go to your meeting, but I got caught up." It essentially negates everything before the *but*, and you are making an excuse about why you didn't make it.

Goal: Be Prepared After the Conversation

The conversation may be over, but the associated work, of course, must continue. Make sure your postconversation plan includes the following exercises so that you and staff are on the same page and progress oriented.

Try This: Summarize and Debrief

Summarize the conversation in a few statements to reflect how you heard the information and to prevent any misunderstandings (Farrell, 2015; Knight, 2016). Next, identify the next steps, specifically any new procedures or requirements. What type of support might they need to be successful? How might you support them? Restate the desired outcome. Was it achieved? Are you both in consensus about it? Reflect together and discuss what you both learned from the conversation. Completing the form in figure 5.3, even if you informally walk through it, might prove useful. (See page 109 for a reproducible version of this figure.)

Summary of Conversation	We determined that what has resulted was never intended. It seemed to get out of hand, and we're not sure how you got to this point.
Next Steps (Any New Procedures or Requirements?)	Roles were explained and clarified, as were misconceptions about expectations for both teachers in the room.
Additional Support Needed?	Yes. More supervision to make sure this doesn't happen in the future as it was going on for a long time and no one noticed or intervened earlier.
Desired Outcome	To maintain cordial relationships between teachers and to support one another when difficulties arise with students.
Was the Desired Outcome Achieved?	Yes. Everything was aired. There were a lot of hurtful actions taken before and intentional things said to be dismissive. Apologies were made and wrong was admitted.
What You Learned From the Conversation	That we should have had this conversation a long time ago.

FIGURE 5.3: Postconversation notes.

VIRTUAL LEARNING LIGHTBULB

Summarizing and debriefing is always a good way to end conversations and larger meetings online as well. In remote settings, there may be connectivity issues or microphone issues or buffering that interferes with messages. There may be different interpretations about what next steps are, and while they might be covered in the desired outcomes of an agenda, it is important to verbally summarize what was accomplished and the next steps to take as a whole with deadlines intact. This will allow room to clarify misunderstandings and time for questions and answers.

Try This: Conduct a Follow-Up or Pulse Check

Remember to not bring up old business. If you hear something down the road that is consistent with what you had a necessary conversation about, try your best not to keep score or hold a grudge (Farrell, 2015). (I keep this one in mind for students too—allow a new day to be a new day!) Be thankful that you had the opportunity to have the conversation, and think about how many *other* necessary conversations you are avoiding. If needed, follow up to this necessary conversation in an email for next steps, and create a timeline for checking in in the future to see how things are going.

School Scenario

Ms. Gladis, a high school teacher leader who was also an instructional coach, did not want to address tardiness with her team because she had heard that one of her teachers was going to come to every meeting deliberately late because she didn't feel their collaborative team meetings were important. Walking through each checklist of questions from before the conversation, she realized she did not know the true desired outcome of the conversation; there was more at stake than people arriving on time, yet she knew she did not want confrontation either. She didn't know where to start. Before she attempted the conversation, she considered asking if she needed any support first.

Conclusion

Using specific before, during, and after strategies to have necessary conversations often results in learning opportunities that enable instructional leaders to address important topics. The most surprising result of approaching necessary conversations is that the outcome is often the complete opposite of the most terrible ending you have imagined (Scott, 2019). We often are afraid of what people will say when we approach them to have a necessary conversation, but people are most often grateful for the opportunity to be heard and have an opportunity to talk things through (Scott, 2019).

Avoiding conversations will rob teachers of the opportunity to be successful in their work (Farrell, 2015). Necessary conversations are ultimately the responsibility of instructional leaders in building ongoing dialogue that will guide staff, encourage accountability, and ultimately build trust (Farrell, 2015). When trust, respect, and clear communication are embodied in norms, teachers are more comfortable sharing ideas and learning from one another (Knight, 2016). Better conversations improve collaboration as there are less hard feelings and more listening, respect, and kindness, which ultimately improve conversations about teaching and learning (Knight, 2016).

The keen ability to recognize that something is not working and take actionable steps toward plausible solutions equates to a mature leader who owns up to their responsibilities in keeping an ongoing dialogue that builds trust and an opportunity for everyone to grow (Farrell, 2015). Instructional leaders often undervalue the emotional labor needed in schools, and it is the necessary conversations you have with guiding teachers where trust is built on a finite level (Scott, 2019). The following reflection questions and action steps invite that emotional labor.

The applicable **Educator Spotlights** in the appendix at the end of the book (page 121) provide examples of real educators involved in this important work.

REFLECTION QUESTIONS

Review and record your responses to the reflection questions so you can refer back to them periodically and track your progress in building trust.

1. What are the sources of conflict at your school? On your team? Between teachers?

2. How can you improve your skills dealing with conflict? What about your team? Your teachers?

3. What norms are in place to address conflict before it happens?

4. Imagine that you could improve the quality of relationships in this school. What would you change, and how might it increase trust in your school?

5. Out of all the tips in this chapter, which one resonates with you the most?

A CHECKLIST OF ACTION STEPS

Check off each of the following items as you complete it.

- ☐ I have identified at least one new strategy to use either before, during, or after a necessary conversation.
- ☐ I am more self-aware of my triggers before initiating a necessary conversation.
- ☐ The strategy I will use to help respond versus react is _____.
- ☐ I have a plan and a person in mind to have a necessary conversation with (either at work or in my personal life).
- ☐ I have someone I can practice necessary conversations with.
- ☐ I have identified at least one coaching mantra to remind myself of through necessary conversations.

Notes for Necessary Conversations

Preparation notes for conversation with _____

Why am I having this conversation?	What is the desired outcome?	How might they react?	How will I respond (not *react*)?

Notes on Where the Conflict Developed and Implications for the School

Notes for conversation with _____ about _____.				
What's the conflict?	What could be the source of the conflict? When did it develop? Write down your perspective.	What are the implications for the school? For the team?	Consider the other person's perspective. What might they say about when the conflict developed and its source?	What are possible solutions?

Postconversation Notes

Summary of Conversation	
Next Steps (Any New Procedures or Requirements?)	
Additional Support Needed?	
Desired Outcome	
Was the Desired Outcome Achieved?	
What You Learned From the Conversation	

CONCLUSION

I sincerely hope that this book has served as a thought partner for you with a positive, how-to approach to move beyond the characteristics of trust toward more intentional, positive, practical, and consistent structures, protocols, and strategies along with reproducible tools for the critical trust-building moments in schools. High levels of trust in schools equate to high levels of performance, and instructional leaders need much more than a directive with numerous examples for how to make this a reality (Finnigan & Daly, 2017; Rensch, 2019; Tschannen-Moran, 2014).

The ability to build trust is a cherished one that makes a significant difference in the lives of teachers in our field with the most incredibly rewarding yet complex career we have chosen. Each chapter focused on ways to build trust on a nuclear level by being more visible and approachable—to be more intentionally present as a leader, to listen closely to the complaint for a request, to invite all voices, to use a strengths-based approach toward building instructional leadership capacity, and to unpack necessary conversations with care.

When teachers feel they have been listened to by their instructional leaders with positive intentions and are able to internalize how to better do their work—judgment suspended—trust increases because teachers know you truly care about them and that you value their work. I look forward to hearing how you make these strategies your own, as all good educators do, and share stories along the way about your journeys. Thank you for allowing me to share mine with you.

APPENDIX

Educator Spotlights

See the following Educator Spotlights for examples of real-world educators who applied the chapter concepts from this book in their own instruction, work communities, and professional development experiences.

CHAPTER 1 EDUCATOR SPOTLIGHTS

Be Visible and Approachable

Jessica M. Dove, *ESOL Instructional Support Teacher for Nontraditional Schools, Fairfax County Public Schools, Virginia*

I work at several different schools, and I must build relationships with colleagues at a number of different sites. I made it a point to visit classrooms very casually when I started. With our coaching team, we used a spreadsheet that was color-coded to identify how we spent our day with specific activities aligned to effective coaching practices (co-planning, classroom observations, leading coaching conversations, pulling small groups, invited classroom observations, teacher-requested coaching conversations, and classroom environmental scan), identifying what types of activities we were doing. It helped me self-assess how I was utilizing my time during the instructional day and how I was intentionally being visible and approachable. This also allowed me to support more teachers, build trust, and cultivate stronger relationships that helped me improve teaching and learning.

I can remember working with a teacher who taught middle school mathematics. He did not have a lot of experience working with English learners and voiced his worries with me about not knowing how to differentiate instruction for ELs with various language proficiencies. He was a mathematics expert, not an EL expert, as he reminded me. I came into his classroom to support ELs, offered support in writing more student-friendly learning targets, and cocreated project-based learning activities that were more hands-on. I remember planning an activity with him to make Rice Krispies treats when the students were learning about fractions. Over time, he felt more comfortable with me, which allowed me to suggest more strategies. He became more comfortable asking me questions when he did not have an approach for a specific student with a difficult concept; he learned that I was approachable. He knew I was always going to show up and would not judge him about how to differentiate instruction for ELs. It was a win-win for us because we did not just coexist in the classroom; we truly co-planned and co-taught, which dramatically improved student achievement. (J. Dove, personal communication, June 21, 2021)

Kendra Chapman, *High School Coordinator, Maury County Public Schools, Columbia, Tennessee*

I have served as an administrator in four different schools in two different states throughout the Southeast. I have also served as an instructional coach, special education teacher, and central office support. I can say, without a doubt, that in each of these roles, being both visible and approachable served me extremely well and, together, were the quickest way to build relationships with a number of educational partners. In reflecting on each of these positions, I can say this has definitely been true, especially within the first ninety days in each new position.

In my most recent role, I was elected to become the new principal. For me, it was a new state in a brand-new division in North Nashville. I spent the first sixty days, at least, building relationships with teachers and community members in this new city. I wanted to know what the community needed, and while I was visible, I listened—a lot! I made sure I was visible and approachable to all educational partners, and when I rethink these first few weeks in this position now, I cannot begin to tell you how much this made a difference for the rest of my 2020–2021 school year.

Most people will reflect on 2020 as the pandemic year; however, I experienced a host of traumatic events even before COVID-19! My school, which I had only spent roughly sixty days in, listening, meeting people, doing learning walks, and building relationships with teachers, suffered severe damage to large portions of the building due to a tornado. Our school was uninhabitable. I had to move buildings to a "new" school within four days, which was shortly followed up by COVID-19, a flip to distance learning overnight, and a complete virtual reopening right after. Had it not been for those relationships that I built those first sixty days in person, I honestly do not think I would have been able to come out of the 2020–2021 school year successfully. I can recall a second-grade teacher sending me an email simply thanking me for being so easy to talk to. She felt I didn't judge her. I treasure these messages because they come from the heart. They represent the type of instructional leader I aim to be and that, in both my visibility and approachability, teachers knew who I really was and that I do care, have high expectations, and really want to listen. I will always look back on these lessons I have learned throughout my career; however, that year in particular and all the valuable takeaways I learned—I hold these memories close. I am so grateful. (K. Chapman, personal communication, September 27, 2021)

CHAPTER 2 EDUCATOR SPOTLIGHTS

Listen Closely to the Complaint for a Request

Melissa Trout, *English Department Chair, Instructional Coach, and Girls Athletic Director; Tustin High School, Tustin Unified School District, California*

This was the game changer for me—learning to listen, especially listening for the request in the complaint. It's been a few years since you [Delia] came to our campus to help us transition to instructional coaches, and while a lot has changed, my team—we are still intact and strong! I am so proud!

The 2020–2021 school year was such a challenge, yet because I learned how to communicate with people before the pandemic, our team continued to consistently support one another during one of the most challenging teaching years in our lifetimes. I am thankful for learning this skill and for building relationships, as it has been a true testament to shifting conversations to keep kids at the core. Our team was not always like this, however. My first year coming into this position . . . I was anxious. I knew this team was volatile. It was passive aggressive—teaching assignments were just handed to us without any conversation—and it was toxic. I remember going into meetings and leaving angry because they were so unproductive. This was our normal. I remember asking my co–department chair, Ryan Miller, "How are we going to put this group back together?" I knew we had to keep our students at the core and keep ourselves out of it. We just didn't know how. Once I learned to listen to what teachers needed, I realized why we were so divided. No one was listening to them! I essentially had to start over with this team. I had to rebuild trust before I could even touch curriculum or lesson planning. I started small and stayed consistent. I made it about people first—my team—and stepped well out of my comfort zone. We weren't enemies—we were on the same team and wanted the same things. Over the course of the year, trust was built, and we started tackling real instructional issues. It became a safe space to discuss common problems. Now my team knows I will advocate for them. Even if they don't get exactly what they want with their teaching assignments, they know they will be listened to and feel supported. That's everything to me and my team. My department, my team—we are more than a team. They are my tribe now, and I am so grateful. (M. Trout, personal communication, June 26, 2021)

Ann Delehant, *Educational Consultant, Delehant and Associates*

Since the early nineties, I have had the privilege of supporting learning with thousands of educators around the United States. I consider myself a facilitator of learning and always begin with a conversation about trust. Trust is a fundamental component of every relationship and is critical in every classroom, every school, and every system in education. Being trustworthy means that I do what I say; I keep my word; I keep what is shared with me confidential, if asked. Being trusting means I have faith in you; I will take a risk with you; I don't have to control everything; I am vulnerable. In order to build trust and be both trustworthy and trusting, we all must learn how to listen to one another, and do so without judgment. Delia reminds us in this particular chapter to listen to one another—listen carefully—and it is what I continually keep at the forefront of my work as a facilitator of instructional leaders.

I remember working with a group of teachers who were in the middle of a conflict with their principal. It was during this argument that the principal turned to one teacher and said, "Oh, I could have predicted *you* would say that." What made it worse is that the teacher she targeted was not the person who'd actually made the comment; she had made an assumption about this teacher's opinion without actually hearing her say those words, and it was a pivotal moment. There were tears, shock, resentment, and anger as the conversations evolved, and it is one conversation that always stays with me when I am reminded of how important it is to listen and speak about *what you actually hear*. Comments like the aforementioned are so small yet make such a significant impact. These types of accusatory comments make a person feel awful; that needs to be acknowledged in future conversations to be able to mend the trust that is broken by such a small yet hurtful accusatory sentence. I am reminded to not only listen carefully but also ensure that what I hear is what a person actually says and appreciate how hurtful unvalidated assumptions can be. (A. Delehant, personal communication, September 27, 2021)

CHAPTER 3 EDUCATOR SPOTLIGHTS

Invite All Voices

Lourdes "Lulu" Amador, *Instructional Coach, North Orange County Regional Occupational Program, California*

This chapter resonates with me so much because when staff come to me with a problem, I have learned that it isn't a personal attack on me. I have built relationships with my teachers, so the way I now see it is they trust me enough to tell me their truth, even when it might sound harsh. When I keep that in mind, it's easy to remember that this complaint is their perspective, not an attack on me.

Our organization is unique. In general, we are partners with our school districts across Orange County. So, when I visit my career and technical education teachers who teach six classes straight without a prep period, I know they barely have a break besides lunch. I remember walking into a culinary class of a teacher who is loved by everyone, and one day, he said to me, "We never get a break! We keep pushing through. I'm an athletic director too, and how am I supposed to get all of this done?"

In that moment, the only thing I knew to do was listen. It is these small moments that matter. Listening builds trust, especially during someone's most challenging moment. It was not about the break or about judgment in that moment. When you are taken over by despair and panic and feel overwhelmed, those five minutes of being listened to matter so very much, and he really needed that break. My simply being there for him in that moment meant everything. How these challenging moments are met mean everything. (L. Amador, personal communication, June 15, 2021)

April Cage, *Principal, Fairfax County Public Schools, Virginia*

I have served as a classroom teacher, advanced academic resource teacher, instructional coach, assistant principal, and principal. I also proudly serve as a mentor to second-year principals. Most of my career has been in Title I schools, and while I have served in affluent schools as well, what I have learned throughout my career is that regardless of the socioeconomic status of the school I am leading, all parents want the same for their children. It is this strong commonality that pushes me to continually improve teaching and learning for all students every day.

Building trust and establishing relationships within any community rise to the top for me. I am passionate about teacher growth and development but am unable to do those things if people do not trust me. I heard a long time ago that "people follow people." That holds true for me, and I know that when teachers say, "I want to be at *that* school," it is because of the people there who care about them. They feel heard, included, and valued.

One example I can recall is at one school where I became a new instructional leader; I followed a veteran principal who had served at this school for fifteen years. It was extremely important not to undo what had been established because the school had been successful before I got there. I made it clear that I was not there to change everything and instead wanted to hear from every educational partner about what really was at the heart of the school. What was important to each of them? I kept it simple and asked that very question: What is the best part of this school, and what is important to you? It was through these dialogues that I was able to deeply learn about what they were most proud of. It was heartwarming. It was each conversation that earned their trust and opened the door to more vulnerable future conversations about what was working and what needed a bit of improvement.

I remember thinking to myself, "Before I got there, they were OK"—and I had to remember that. I also had to find out how they made it OK and who all was involved. I had to speak to everyone. I wanted to tap into that historical knowledge. I knew that the reason that principal was successful wasn't because they did the work alone. This process of finding out the *who* and the *what* really allowed me room to build strong relationships. I also respected the fact that not everyone was happy the previous principal was gone—they missed my predecessor. It was important for me to not bash my predecessor for anything that did come up that wasn't working well.

My journey at this school was such a successful one that started by genuinely being interested in what each person's experiences were and including everyone's voice to be heard, whether community members, parents, or office staff. Their voices were included in the strategic plan for the school, and we succeeded in increasing scores across the board by the end of my tenure at that school. Beyond scores, we trusted each other. They trusted me. We valued what we each had to share, and that is how our kids soared. (A. Cage, personal communication, October 5, 2021)

CHAPTER 4 EDUCATOR SPOTLIGHTS
Use a Strengths-Based Approach Toward Building Instructional Leadership Capacity

Rae Mitchell, *Executive Director, Chief of Schools for Loudoun County Public Schools, Loudoun, Virginia*

As a previous instructional coach, administrator, and now executive director, I can relate to everything about this chapter—really this entire book—but specifically with regard to building capacity in instructional leaders, as well as leaders-to-be. There are so many skills you want to empower your leaders to have—how to lead, what to look for in classrooms—and you ultimately need to build their independence so they can teach other teachers how to do the same in turn.

For me, all this work is connected to trust. I myself am not going to lean into you if I don't trust you. Yet to be trusted, you must be vulnerable. You must learn to trust with vulnerability, and that's hard. Trust is earned and is a vital element in building capacity.

What keeps coming to the forefront for me now, as I reflect on trust and building instructional leadership capacity, is an experience I had with another instructional leader. He had a lot of great qualities to be a leader. He was a relationship builder, constantly confident about everything—in a good way. His work ethic was strong. He was a good listener. He wanted to diligently consider all perspectives before putting something into action. Yet the focus was to build his instructional capacity, and we were going to do that together. I had to take time to build a relationship with him first to be able to identify his strengths and his perspective, and I was cognizant to not discredit any of his ideas to be able to merge our visions together. And we did. I see that I built instructional leadership through each conversation about his strengths with him. It was because of the trust that we had between each other that we were able to extend it to our teachers. We trusted, and therefore trust was extended back to us. When I look back, I recognize the power in having utilized a strengths-based approach in building instructional leadership capacity and its relationship to building trust. (R. Mitchell, personal communication, June 14, 2021)

Brittany Hott, *Associate Professor of Special Education, Department of Educational Psychology, University of Oklahoma; Assessment and Evaluation Consultant for PreK–12 Schools; Former Special Education Teacher and Administrator*

I am currently an associate professor of special education with more than twenty years of service in both higher education and preK–12 schools. I have served as a special education teacher, alternative education teacher, and administrator of special education, mostly in rural and urban areas. This particular chapter is one that aligns well with me because there are so many myths, particularly about rural education and rural communities, that impact our students and must be dispelled. I am extremely fortunate to work with valuable instructional leaders throughout our community who each serve in unique roles where their strengths are leveraged to further support other instructional leaders, and ultimately students, with a range of unique needs. It is, in a sense, a very large multiplier effect in the rural communities I serve—all rooted in a strengths-based approach.

One example of this type of support starts with the strong relationships that are quite insular within many rural communities I work with. I work with more than nine districts that are all joined to best serve all their districts collectively. Often in rural communities, one person serves numerous roles and needs access to an expert; however, that role or position does not exist in their district to provide support, nor do they have a model to work with to support a specific student or group of students. For example, I recently met a speech pathologist in one of my nine districts who has a vast amount of experience that I knew another district needed to support a group of students with special needs, and through this co-op approach, we were able to break down the silo of her direct district and support a number of additional students. COVID-19 opened up this opportunity, and we were able to support districts in reconsidering how they were offering services to students.

In my role as a professor and as an assessment consultant with preK–12 students, I am able to build a network of expertise, based on the strengths of each individual instructional leader, to meet the needs of multiple students. Even if it is not with a specific service, it is with specific expertise that helps that student. We have been able to not only identify people as resources but also pull together an inventory of resources available to each district to better assess what we were each using and why to support our students. This process further was drilled down to specific strategies that worked and how they were used as well.

This multiplier effect has expanded the vast experience and expertise across nine districts—something I am so grateful for that would not have worked without this type of large-scale strengths-based approach. Now our districts have a wealth of people to lean on, and it has been extremely helpful during these extremely challenging times as instructional leaders also need instructional leaders. (B. Hott, personal communication, September 27, 2021)

Melissa Ferro, *English Language Instructor, University of Texas at Austin*

I have served as a language instructor for twenty years and a teacher educator for ten years—and both roles, fortunately, in the United States and the United Kingdom. My career has focused on building trust through building on the strengths with teachers, as well as the students they work with, to continually improve teaching and learning.

What I have learned throughout my career is that to build instructional capacity, I have to do a lot of homework before I go into a new school or organization. I also think it is always important for educators to know that I want what is best for them and am genuinely interested in what they feel they are already good at doing in the classroom. My passion has remained constant throughout my career, and that is working with beginning teachers because they bring so much to the table already, and I enjoy helping them discover their strengths.

Trust building takes time, however, especially when you are tasked with "fixing" a program. When I moved to the UK, I didn't really know what I didn't know yet. I had a lot to learn not only about a different educational system but about one in a new country. However, what stayed constant for me was my approach and focusing on the strengths of teachers first and also knowing that although I was hired to fix a program, I believe in building people, not fixing them, and that's the approach I decided to take.

I was hired as an academic developer to better align the program design, yet I had to first learn all the differences in how programs were aligned to begin with! I had to understand a lot of tradition and history while also balancing the realities of global competitiveness and knowing what our students were up against, particularly on a global scale. What better place to begin learning than with a small group of teachers? I learned as much as I could from them, particularly learning about their strengths and their dreams and what they were already good at. We started there and collectively identified similar areas to focus on, which developed into one-hour workshops, and kept our goals small and practical. I used the group to grow the group, in essence. I found great success with this approach, all focused around their strengths, versus the requested deficit approach. Instead of focusing on what was wrong, we focused on what was right and what was going well. There was also a significant sharing of cultural understanding, and once I realized that I could tap into their current strengths and identify their significantly strong potential, it was this mindset that shifted learning for everyone. From that moment on, as a collective group of instructional leaders, we started our journey of improving teaching and learning together. Did we figure out all solutions? No. Did we shift mindset? Yes! We started the journey of continuous improvement together—we could feel it—and that experience will always stay with me as an instructional leader. (M. Ferro, personal communication, October 6, 2021)

CHAPTER 5 EDUCATOR SPOTLIGHTS
Unpack Necessary Conversations With Care

Breána Victoria, *Elementary School Teacher; Mentor Teacher; and Doctoral Student at Chapman University*

I am currently a kindergarten teacher, a mentor teacher for preservice teachers, and a doctoral student at Chapman University. I have really taken this chapter to heart because it aligns with what I am working on personally right now—everything about having necessary conversations. What resonates with me in every corner of my life right now is that we have to actually start humanizing each other. We are all so quick to judge each other today, and many conversations that must be had are avoided because it's easier and we don't want to say anything "wrong" or offensive, especially nowadays. But we are not going to grow if we don't. These conversations are necessary so that we can learn, unlearn, and relearn so that we can all do better for society.

One specific scenario I recall is working with my mentee who observes in my classroom during the day at school. She was given an assignment to identify a "low-performing" student, and she was really anxious about the lack of progress a few students were making during the year of the global pandemic. I reminded her that standards were the expectation for the end of the year, not this current moment, and reminded her that they would get there but that, for purposes of this assignment, we would identify a student who was performing below grade-level standards. I realized in that moment that I had already made an assumption about this assignment because of the verbiage that was chosen for her to pick a student, yet I had to make sure that I was truly mentoring this preservice student, so I shifted my mindset a bit to assume positive intentions and coach her—truly coach her. Her assignment was to come up with a letter-and-sound activity for this student in kindergarten, and she had to include a culturally and linguistically diverse approach. She was transparent and told me she had no idea what that even meant. I decided to coach her by leading with questions in this moment and started with a question and asked, "What do you think you should do?" to try to figure out where she was exactly and, again, avoid any assumptions.

I must admit I was taken back. I knew she was having trouble in this area; however, I, too, had been avoiding it. So, after pitching out the first question and identifying that she did not know, I decided to switch roles and highlight some key strengths about English learners instead. I realized as I was explaining this to her that I was teaching her how to not make assumptions about her own students. I gave her ideas, for example, to think about images or pictures that students might be able to relate to or identify with and to take that into account. She was receptive to the input. I realized I had planted many seeds, and I'm glad she told me she simply didn't know. The conversation ended up going differently than I had envisioned, and I, too, learned to assume more positive intentions next time. (B. Victoria, personal communication, June 10, 2021)

Nadya Briggs, *Assistant Principal, Montgomery County Public Schools, Maryland*

I am currently an assistant principal, entering my third year leading an elementary school. I have served as an instructional coach and an alternative education and intervention teacher with a passion for advocating for the underdog in and out of education. In my core, I truly believe that with the right support and instruction, all students can thrive. It is truly the center of my why for what I do. Through my work as a coach and administrator, I have learned to keep my same belief and drive about adults while keeping my work centered around what is best for kids.

When a conversation needs to happen, I constantly remind myself that my number one priority is children. I want to ensure that what I want for my own children I advocate for all children I serve. I also heavily consider how I want to be approached when I know I have to have a necessary conversation with someone else. I want honesty; however, I also want grace and compassion.

The person who keeps coming to mind for me when I think about having necessary conversations is a teacher I used to work with who was deemed "mean." She was instructionally sound; however, she appeared to be missing empathy, patience, and compassion—to me, the essence of teaching. I remember taking the time to show her that I cared but not at the expense of my core beliefs. I knew that everyone thought she was mean, but I always knew it had to stem from somewhere for her, and for some reason, I had to figure out why because I knew it was what was best for kids. I always gave her the truth—what I wanted someone to tell me—while being transparent, always with the belief that she could do better, and supported her along her journey. It was important to me to not simply tell her to get better but walk beside her while she grew, showing her examples of what specifically she was doing or not doing to help her grow and further identifying how to shift her behavior. She referred to herself as not having an "empathy gene," and yet I had to show her how to build relationships and more importantly help her see her strengths and build on them first. She trusted me over time because I was able to show her what she was doing that reflected what she could become. It was always there. She was phenomenal in instruction; in essence, I knew that was her strength, yet she really needed to learn how to build relationships with all of her students, not just the compliant ones, so they could take in all she had to offer. I'll always remember what she said to me: "We don't always agree, but you will always listen to what I have to say and tell me your honest thoughts." This is the essence of having necessary conversations and ultimately benefited the students who needed her instructional strengths the most. (N. Briggs, personal communication, September 23, 2021)

REFERENCES AND RESOURCES

Abaya, J., & Normore, A. H. (2014). The contextual impact on school leadership in Kenya and need for trust formation. *Planning and Changing, 45*(3–4), 285–310.

Abrams, J. (2009). *Having hard conversations.* Thousand Oaks, CA: Corwin Press.

Abrams, J. (2016). *Hard conversations unpacked: The whos, the whens, and the what-ifs.* Thousand Oaks, CA: Corwin Press.

Adams, C. M. (2013). Collective trust: A social indicator of instructional capacity. *Journal of Educational Administration, 51*(3), 363–382.

Anderson, K. (n.d.). *Presuming positive intent and positive presuppositions* [Blog post]. Accessed at http://resultscoachingglobal.com/presuming-positive-intent-and-positive-presuppositions/on April 18, 2022.

Arneson, S. M. (2015). *Building trust in teacher evaluations: It's not what you say, it's how you say it.* Thousand Oaks, CA: Corwin Press.

AVID Center. (2017). *Helping trios for students* [Protocol]. San Diego, CA: Author.

Bennis, W., & Goldsmith, J. (2010). *Learning to lead: A workbook on becoming a leader* (4th ed.). New York: Basic Books.

Berger, W. (2014). *A more beautiful question: The power of inquiry to spark breakthrough ideas.* New York: Bloomsbury.

Bezzina, C. (2006). "The road less traveled": Professional learning communities in secondary schools. *Theory Into Practice, 45*(2), 159–167.

Bloom, G., Castagna, C., Moir, E., & Warren, B. (2005). *Blended coaching: Skills and strategies to support principal development.* Thousand Oaks, CA: Corwin Press.

Brownell, J. (2018). *Listening: Attitudes, principles, and skills* (6th ed.). New York: Routledge.

Bryk, A. S., Sebring, P. B., Allensworth, E., Luppescu, S., & Easton, J. Q. (2010). *Organizing schools for improvement: Lessons from Chicago.* Chicago: University of Chicago Press.

Cain, S. (2012). *Quiet: The power of introverts in a world that can't stop talking.* New York: Crown.

Collins, M. (2021, March 3). *Attention school leaders: Listening is essential. Here's how to get better at it.* Accessed at www.edsurge.com/news/2021–03–03-attention-school-leaders-listening-is-essential-here-s-how-to-get-better-at-it#:~:text=Listening%20allows%20us%20insight%20about,help%20educators%20work%20more%20collaboratively.&text=As%20a%20school%20leader%2C%20it,people%20to%20get%20in%20touch on October 14, 2021.

Costa, A. L., & Garmston, R. J. (2016). *Cognitive coaching: Developing self-directed leaders and learners* (3rd ed.). Lanham, MD: Rowman & Littlefield.

Covey, S. M. R. (2018). *The speed of trust: The one thing that changes everything.* New York: Simon & Schuster.

Craig, W. (2018, October 23). The nature of leadership in a flat organization. *Forbes.* Accessed at www.forbes.com/sites/williamcraig/2018/10/23/the-nature-of-leadership-in-a-flat-organization on October 14, 2021.

Crowther, F. (2011). *From school improvement to sustained capacity: The parallel leadership pathway.* Thousand Oaks, CA: Corwin Press.

Daly, A. J., Moolenaar, N. M., Liou, Y-H., Tuytens, M., & del Fresno, M. (2015). Why so difficult? Exploring negative relationships between educational leaders: The role of trust, climate, and efficacy. *American Journal of Education, 122*(1), 1–38.

de Jong, B. A., Dirks, K. T., & Gillespie, N. (2016). Trust and team performance: A meta-analysis of main effects, moderators, and covariates. *Journal of Applied Psychology, 101*(8), 1134–1150.

Devos, G., Tuytens, M., & Hulpia, H. (2014). Teachers' organizational commitment: Examining the mediating effects of distributed leadership. *American Journal of Education, 120*(2), 205–231.

DeWitt, P. (2015, February 17). Being visible isn't enough. *Education Week.* Accessed at www.edweek.org/education/opinion-being-visible-isnt-enough/2015/02 on October 15, 2021.

DeWitt, P. M. (2022). *Collective leader efficacy: Strengthening instructional leadership teams.* Thousand Oaks, CA: Corwin Press.

Doshi, N., & McGregor, L. (2015). *Primed to perform: How to build the highest performing cultures through the science of total motivation.* New York: HarperCollins.

DuFour, R., DuFour, R., Eaker, R., Many, T. W., & Mattos, M. (2016). *Learning by doing: A handbook for Professional Learning Communities at Work* (3rd ed.). Bloomington, IN: Solution Tree Press.

Ellis, D. (2002). *Falling awake: Creating the life of your dreams.* San Rafael, CA: Breakthrough Enterprises.

Eriksen, M. (2009). Authentic leadership: Practical reflexivity, self-awareness, and self-authorship. *Journal of Management Education, 33*(6), 747–771.

Farrell, M. (2015). Difficult conversations. *Journal of Library Administration, 55*(4), 302–311.

Fauville, G., Luo, M., Queiroz, A. C. M., Bailenson, J. N., & Hancock, J. (2021). Zoom Exhaustion & Fatigue Scale. *Computers in Human Behavior Reports, 4.* Accessed at https://www.sciencedirect.com/science/article/pii/S2451958821000671 on May 3, 2022.

Ferlazzo, L. (2018, April 28). Response: Being a principal means "spending time each day building relationships." *Education Week.* Accessed at www.edweek.org/leadership/opinion-response-being-a-principal-means-spending-time-each-day-building-relationships/2018/04 on October 15, 2021.

Finnigan, K. S., & Daly, A. J. (2017). The trust gap: Understanding the effects of leadership churn in school districts. *American Educator, 41*(2), 24–29, 43.

Fisher, D., & Frey, N. (2019). Listening stations in content area learning. *Reading Teacher, 72*(6), 769–773.

Fisher, D., Frey, N., & Hattie, J. (2020). *The distance learning playbook, grades K–12: Teaching for engagement and impact in any setting.* Thousand Oaks, CA: Corwin Press.

Forner, M., Bierlein-Palmer, L., & Reeves, P. (2012). Leadership practices of effective rural superintendents: Connections to Waters and Marzano's leadership correlates. *Journal of Research in Rural Education, 27*(8).

Forsyth, P. B., Adams, C. M., & Hoy, W. K. (2011). *Collective trust: Why schools can't improve without it.* New York: Teachers College Press.

Frazier, R. A. (2021). *The joy of coaching: Characteristics of effective instructional coaches.* Thousand Oaks, CA: Corwin Press.

Fullan, M. (2014). *The principal: Three keys to maximizing impact.* San Francisco: Jossey-Bass.

Fullan, M. (2016). *The new meaning of educational change* (5th ed.). New York: Teachers College Press.

Fullan, M. (2019). *Nuance: Why some leaders succeed and others fail.* Thousand Oaks, CA: Corwin Press.

Fullan, M., & Quinn, J. (2016a). *Coherence: The right drivers in action for schools, districts, and systems.* Thousand Oaks, CA: Corwin Press.

Fullan, M., & Quinn, J. (2016b). Coherence-making: How leaders cultivate the pathway for school and system change with a shared process. *School Administrator.* Accessed at http://prism.scholarslab.org/prisms/ff97698e-659f-11e7-b13a-005056b3784e/visualize?locale=en on October 15, 2021.

Garmston, R. J., & Wellman, B. M. (2016). *The adaptive school: A sourcebook for developing collaborative groups* (3rd ed.). Lanham, MD: Rowman & Littlefield.

Gladwell, M. (2019). *Talking to strangers: What we should know about the people we don't know.* New York: Little, Brown.

Golembiewski, R. T., & McConkie, M. (1975). The centrality of interpersonal trust in group processes. In C. L. Cooper (Ed.), *Theories of group processes* (pp. 131–185). New York: Wiley.

Graham, P., & Ferriter, W. M. (2010). *Building a Professional Learning Community at Work: A guide to the first year.* Bloomington, IN: Solution Tree Press.

Grissom, J. A., Loeb, S., & Master, B. (2013). Effective instructional time use for school leaders: Longitudinal evidence from observations of principals. *Educational Researcher, 42*(8), 433–444.

Harrison, D., Ziegler, B., & Sackey, A. (2021). Roundtable: The hard conversations—February 2021. *Principal Leadership, 21*(6), 26–33.

Horton, D. M. (2017). *Leading school teams: Building trust to promote student learning.* Thousand Oaks, CA: Corwin Press.

Johnston, W. R., & Berglund, T. (2018). *The prevalence of collaboration among American teachers: National findings from the American Teacher Panel.* Accessed at www.rand.org/pubs/research_reports/RR2217.html on October 15, 2021.

Joshi, A., Lazarova, M. B., & Liao, H. (2009). Getting everyone on board: The role of inspirational leadership in geographically dispersed teams. *Organization Science, 20*(1), 240–252.

Kaur, V. (2020). *See no stranger: A memoir and manifesto of revolutionary love.* New York: One World.

Kets de Vries, M. F. R., Korotov, K., Florent-Treacy, E., & Rook, C. (Eds.). (2016). *Coach and couch: The psychology of making better leaders* (2nd ed.). Houndmills, Basingstoke, Hampshire: Palgrave Macmillan.

Klein, A. (2021, October 5). How much screen time is too much? The answer is 'it depends.' *Education Week.* Accessed at https://www.edweek.org/technology/how-much-screen-time-is-too-much-the-answer-is-it-depends/2021/10 on January 14, 2022.

Knight, J. (2016). *Better conversations: Coaching ourselves and each other to be more credible, caring, and connected.* Thousand Oaks, CA: Corwin Press.

Knight, J. (2017, January 17). *Listening* [Blog post]. Accessed at www.instructionalcoaching.com /listening-2/ on October 15, 2021.

Knight, J. (2018). *The impact cycle: What instructional coaches should do to foster powerful improvements in teaching.* Thousand Oaks, CA: Corwin Press.

Knight, J. (2021, December 6). *The learning zone / Should coaches be experts?* Accessed at https://www.ascd.org/el/articles/the-learning-zone-should-coaches-be-experts on January 27, 2022.

Knight, J., Knight, J. R., & Carlson, C. (2017). *The reflection guide to the impact cycle: What instructional coaches should do to foster powerful improvements in teaching.* Thousand Oaks, CA: Corwin Press.

Knudson, J. (2013). *You'll never be better than your teachers: The Garden Grove approach to human capital development.* Washington, DC: American Institutes for Research.

Kouzes, J. M., & Posner, B. Z. (2017). *The leadership challenge: How to make extraordinary things happen in organizations* (6th ed.). Hoboken, NJ: Wiley.

Kutsyuruba, B., Walker, K., & Noonan, B. (2016). The trust imperative in the school principalship: The Canadian perspective. *Leadership and Policy in Schools, 15*(3), 343–372.

Lewis, C. C., & Hurd, J. (2011). *Lesson study step by step: How teacher learning communities improve instruction.* Portsmouth, NH: Heinemann.

Li, L., Hallinger, P., & Walker, A. (2016). Exploring the mediating effects of trust on principal leadership and teacher professional learning in Hong Kong primary schools. *Educational Management Administration and Leadership, 44*(1), 20–42.

Maister, D. H., Green, C. H., & Galford, R. M. (2000). *The trusted advisor.* New York: Simon & Schuster.

Malik, M. (2016). Assessment of a professional development program on adult learning theory. *Libraries and the Academy, 16*(1), 47–70.

Manna, P. (2015). *Developing excellent school principals to advance teaching and learning: Considerations for state policy.* New York: Wallace Foundation.

Marks, M., & Printy, M. (2003). Principal leadership and school performance: An integration of transformational and instructional leadership. *Educational Administration Quarterly, 39*(3), 370-397.

Martin, R., O'Hara, S., Bookmyer, J., & Newton, R. (2020). Identifying high-impact practices of learning communities that foster collective professional growth. *New Educator, 16*(4), 296–312.

Martin, R. L., & Osberg, S. R. (2015). *Getting beyond better: How social entrepreneurship works.* Boston: Harvard Business Review Press.

Marzano, R. J. (2011). The art & science of teaching: Making the most of instructional rounds. *Educational Leadership, 68*(5), 80–82.

Marzano, R. J., Pickering, D. J., & Pollock, J. E. (2001). *Classroom instruction that works: Research-based strategies for increasing student achievement.* Alexandria, VA: Association for Supervision and Curriculum Development.

Maxwell, J. C. (2010). *Everyone communicates, few connect: What the most effective people do differently.* Nashville, TN: Thomas Nelson.

Maxwell, J. C. (2019). *Leadershift: The 11 essential changes every leader must embrace.* Nashville, TN: HarperCollins Leadership.

May, H., Huff, J., & Goldring, E. (2012). A longitudinal study of principals' activities and student performance. *School Effectiveness and School Improvement, 23*(4), 417–439.

McKenzie, K. B., & Locke, L. A. (2014). Distributed leadership: A good theory but what if leaders won't, don't know how, or can't lead? *Journal of School Leadership, 24*(1), 164–188.

McLain, B. (2011). Conflict is normal, but learning to deal with conflict skillfully takes practice. *Journal of Staff Development, 32*(2), 60–61.

Morris, L. V. (2014). Who's listening? *Innovative Higher Education, 39*, 1–2.

Munby, H., & Russell, T. (1994). The authority of experience in learning to teach: Messages from a physics methods class. *Journal of Teacher Education, 45*(2), 86–95.

Murphy, K. (2020). *You're not listening: What you're missing and why it matters.* New York: Celadon Books.

National Association of Secondary School Principals. (2020, May 14). *With nearly half of principals considering leaving, research urges attention to working conditions, compensation, and supports.* Accessed at www.nassp.org/news/with-nearly-half-of-principals-considering-leaving-research-urges-attention-to-working-conditions-compensation-and-supports/ on October 15, 2021.

Neumerski, C. M. (2013). Rethinking instructional leadership, a review: What do we know about principal, teacher, and coach instructional leadership, and where should we go from here? *Educational Administration Quarterly, 49*(2), 310–347.

Neumerski, C. M., Grissom, J. A., Goldring, E., Rubin, M., Cannata, M., Schuermann, P., et al. (2018). Restructuring instructional leadership: How multiple-measure teacher evaluation systems are redefining the role of the school principal. *Elementary School Journal, 119*(2), 270–297.

Nguyen, T. D., & Hunter, S. B. (2018, January). Towards an understanding of dynamics among teachers, teacher leaders, and administrators in a teacher-led school reform. *Journal of Educational Change, 19*, 539–565.

Ofgang, E. (2021, April). Why Zoom fatigue occurs and how educators can overcome it. *Tech and Learning*, 37–38.

Ontario Principals' Council. (2011). *The principal as leader of challenging conversations.* Thousand Oaks, CA: Corwin Press.

Penuel, W. R., Riel, M., Joshi, A., Pearlman, L., Kim, C. M., & Frank, K. A. (2010). The alignment of the informal and formal organizational supports for reform: Implications for improving teaching in schools. *Educational Administration Quarterly, 46*(1), 57–95.

Peregoy, S. F., & Boyle, O. F. (2017). *Reading, writing, and learning in ESL: A resource book for teaching K–12 English learners* (7th ed.). Boston: Pearson.

Petrilli, M. J. (2021, April 14). Pandemic recovery will be complex. We'll need the best school leaders. *Education Week*. Accessed at www.edweek.org/leadership/opinion-pandemic -recovery-will-be-complex-well-need-the-best-school-leaders/2021/04 on October 15, 2021.

Portin, B. S., Knapp, M. S., Dareff, S., Feldman, S., Russell, F. A., Samuelson, C., et al. (2009). *Leadership for learning improvement in urban schools*. Seattle, WA: Center for the Study of Teaching and Policy. Accessed at https://www.wallacefoundation.org/knowledge-center/Documents /Leadership-for-Learning-Improvement-in-Urban-Schools.pdf on April 19, 2022.

Prestine, N. A., & Nelson, B. S. (2005). How can educational leaders support and promote teaching and learning? New conceptions of learning and leading in schools. In W. A. Firestone & C. Riehl (Eds.), *A new agenda for research in educational leadership* (pp. 46–60). New York: Teachers College Press.

Quaglia, R. J., & Corso, M. J. (2014). Student voice: Pump it up. *Principal Leadership, 15*(1), 28–32.

Racines, D. (2019, August 23). *4 tips for instructional coaches*. Accessed at www.edutopia.org/ article/4-tips-instructional-coaches on October 15, 2021.

Racines, D. E. (2016). *Using self-study to advance research in TESOL teacher education: Examining my EL identity to improve my effectiveness as an instructional coach with teachers of ELs*. Accessed at http://newsmanager.commpartners.com/tesolteis/issues/2016-09-08/2.html on October 15, 2021.

Ramey, M. D. (2015). Supporting a new generation of early childhood professionals. *Young Children, 70*(2), 6–9.

Razer, M., & Friedman, V. J. (2017). *From exclusion to excellence: Building restorative relationships to create inclusive schools*. Cambridge, MA: Birkhäuser Boston.

Reeves, D. (2009). *Leading change in your school: How to conquer myths, build commitment, and get results*. Alexandria, VA: Association for Supervision and Curriculum Development.

Reeves, D. (2021). *Deep change leadership: A model for renewing and strengthening schools and districts*. Bloomington, IN: Solution Tree Press.

Rensch, T. (2019, May 29). Balancing trust and power in your school. *Corwin Connect*. Accessed at https://corwin-connect.com/2019/05/balancing-trust-and-power-in-your-school/ on October 15, 2021.

Riordan, C. M. (2014, January 16). Three ways leaders can listen with more empathy. *Harvard Business Review*. Accessed at https://hbr.org/2014/01/three-ways-leaders-can-listen-with- more-empathy on October 15, 2021.

Robert, L. P., Jr., & You, S. (2018). Are you satisfied yet? Shared leadership, individual trust, autonomy, and satisfaction in virtual teams. *Journal of the Association for Information Science and Technology, 69*(4), 503–513.

Rotter, J. B. (1967). A new scale for the measurement of interpersonal trust. *Journal of Personality, 35*(4), 651–665.

Samaras, A. (2011). *Self-study teacher research: Improving your practice through collaborative inquiry*. Thousand Oaks, CA: SAGE.

Saphier, J. (2018). Let's get specific about how leaders can build trust. *Learning Professional, 39*(6), 14–16.

Sawchuk, S. (2020, October 13). 5 ways principals can establish a strong school climate. *Education Week.* Accessed at www.edweek.org/leadership/5-ways-principals-can-establish-a -strong-school-climate/2020/10 on October 15, 2021.

School Reform Initiative. (2021). *Consultancy protocol: Framing consultancy dilemmas.* Denver, CO: Author.

Scott, K. (2019). *Radical candor: Be a kick-ass boss without losing your humanity* (Rev. and updated ed.). New York: St. Martin's Press.

Scott, S. (2017). *Fierce conversations: Achieving success at work & in life, one conversation at a time.* New York: New American Library.

Scribner, S. P., & Crow, G. M. (2012). Employing professional identities: Case study of a high school principal in a reform setting. *Leadership and Policy in Schools, 11*(3), 243–274.

Seidman, I. (2019). *Interviewing as qualitative research: A guide for researchers in education and the social sciences* (5th ed.). New York: Teachers College Press.

Soehner, C. B., & Darling, A. (2017). *Effective difficult conversations: A step-by-step guide.* Chicago: ALA Editions.

Stanier, M. B. (2016). *The coaching habit: Say less, ask more & change the way you lead forever.* Toronto, Ontario, Canada: Box of Crayons Press.

Sue, D. W. (2015). *Race talk and the conspiracy of silence: Understanding and facilitating difficult dialogues on race.* Hoboken, NJ: Wiley.

Superville, D. R. (2019, June 25). Advice for new principals: Be 'emotionally vulnerable with your staff.' *Education Week.* Accessed at www.edweek.org/leadership/advice-for-new-principals-be -emotionally-vulnerable-with-your-staff/2019/06 on October 15, 2021.

Supovitz, J. A. (2018). Teacher leaders' work with peers in a quasi-formal teacher leadership model. *School Leadership and Management, 38*(1), 53–79.

Toll, C. A. (2018). Progress in literacy coaching success: A dozen years on. *Clearing House, 91*(1), 14–20.

Torres, M. W. (2010). Conversation protocols help district discuss all sides of complicated issues. *Journal of Staff Development, 31*(4), 63–64.

Tschannen-Moran, M. (2014). *Trust matters: Leadership for successful schools* (2nd ed.). San Francisco: Jossey-Bass.

Turner, E. S. (2010). *A correlational study of trust in an organization undergoing change* [Doctoral dissertation, University of Phoenix]. ProQuest. Accessed at www.proquest.com/openview/39 f1da6de56323015a3d50ff9c755227/1?pq-origsite=gscholar&cbl=18750 on April 20, 2022.

Twaronite, K. (2016, July 22). A global survey on the ambiguous state of employee trust. *Harvard Business Review.* Accessed at https://hbr.org/2016/07/a-global-survey-on-the-ambiguous- state-of-employee-trust on October 15, 2021.

van de Loo, E. (2016). The art of listening. In M. F. R. Kets de Vries, K. Korotov, E. Florent-Treacy, & C. Rook (Eds.), *Coach and couch: The psychology of making better leaders* (2nd ed., pp. 121–137). Houndmills, Basingstoke, Hampshire: Palgrave Macmillan.

Weiner, J., & Woulfin, S. L. (2018). Sailing across the divide: Challenges to the transfer of teacher leadership. *Journal of Research on Leadership Education, 13*(3), 210–234.

Wieczorek, D., & Lear, J. (2018). Building the "bridge": Teacher leadership for learning and distributed organizational capacity for instructional improvement. *International Journal of Teacher Leadership, 9*(2), 22–47.

Wieczorek, D., & Manard, C. (2018). Instructional leadership challenges and practices of novice principals in rural schools. *Journal of Research in Rural Education, 34*(2).

Will, M. (2019, October 15). 4 things principals can do (and 4 things they shouldn't) to build relationships with teachers. *Education Week.* Accessed at www.edweek.org/leadership/4-things -principals-can-do-and-4-things-they-shouldnt-to-build-relationships-with-teachers/2019/10 on October 15, 2021.

Willis, J. (2018, July 13). The value of active listening. *Edutopia.* Accessed at www.edutopia.org /article/value-active-listening on October 15, 2021.

Youngs, P., & King, M. B. (2002). Principal leadership for professional development to build school capacity. *Educational Administration Quarterly, 38*(5), 643–670.

INDEX

Everyday Instructional Coaching
Nathan D. Lang-Raad

Discover seven drivers you can use to improve your daily coaching practices: collaboration, transparency, inquiry, discourse, reverberation, sincerity, and influence. Each of the book's chapters defines, describes, and offers tips for implementing one of the seven drivers.
BKF802

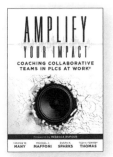

Amplify Your Impact
Thomas W. Many, Michael J. Maffoni, Susan K. Sparks, and Tesha Ferriby Thomas

Now is the time to improve collaboration in your PLC. Using the latest research on coaching and collaboration, the authors share concrete action steps your school can take to adopt proven collaborative coaching methods, fortify teacher teams, and ultimately improve student learning in classrooms.
BKF794

Educator Wellness
Timothy D. Kanold and Tina H. Boogren

How do we bring our best selves to our students and colleagues each day? Designed as a reflective journal and guidebook, _Educator Wellness_ will take you on a deep exploration where you will uncover profound answers that ring true for you.
BKG053

From Burnt Out to Fired Up
Morgane Michael

Overwhelmed teachers, this book is for you. The truth is that you can be remarkable without burning out. Drawing from the latest research and her own teaching experiences, author Morgane Michael delivers research-backed strategies to replenish your well-being and reignite your passion for your purpose.
BKG027

Solution Tree | Press   _a division of_
                           Solution Tree

Visit SolutionTree.com or call 800.733.6786 to order.

Wait! Your professional development journey doesn't have to end with the last pages of this book.

We realize improving student learning doesn't happen overnight. And your school or district shouldn't be left to puzzle out all the details of this process alone.

No matter where you are on the journey, we're committed to helping you get to the next stage.

Take advantage of everything from **custom workshops** to **keynote presentations** and **interactive web and video conferencing**. We can even help you develop an action plan tailored to fit your specific needs.

Let's get the conversation started.

Call 888.763.9045 today.